The
Investigation
of Buildings

W.W. NORTON & COMPANY LTD
10 Coptic Street, London WC1A 1PU
Telephone: 020-7323 1579. Fax: 020-7436 4553
e-mail: ariadne@wwnorton.co.uk

REVIEW COPY

THE INVESTIGATION OF BUILDINGS
A Guide for Architects, Engineers, and Owners

Donald Friedman

Publication date	September 2000
Price	£25.00

A Norton Professional Book for Architects and Designers

Please send two copies of your review. *Thank you.*

For further information please contact Ariadne van de Ven

The Investigation of Buildings

Donald Friedman

W. W. NORTON & COMPANY
New York • London

ALSO BY DONALD FRIEDMAN

Historical Building Construction
The Design of Renovations (with Nathaniel Oppenheimer)
Building the Empire State (edited by Carol Willis)

While precautions have been taken to ensure that all data and information furnished are as accurate as possible, the author and publisher cannot assume responsibility for errors or for the interpretation of the information. The data given here cannot replace the judgment of an experienced structural engineer familiar with the overall requirements involved during testing, design, and detailing.

A NORTON PROFESSIONAL BOOK

For information about permission to reproduce selections from this book, write to Permissions, W. W. Norton & Company, Inc., 500 Fifth Avenue, New York, NY 10110

The text of this book is composed in New Caledonia
with the display set in Gill Sans
Manufacturing by Thomson-Shore, Inc.
Book design by Gilda Hannah

Photographs courtesy of LZA Technology, a division of the Thornton-Tomasetti Group

Library of Congress Cataloging-in-Publication Data
Friedman, Donald.
    The investigation of buildings / Donald Friedman.
       p. cm.
    "A Norton professional book."
    Includes index.
    ISBN 0-393-73054-9
    1. Building inspection. I. Title.
TH439 .F75 2000
690—dc21   00-029184

W. W. Norton & Company, Inc., 500 Fifth Avenue, New York, NY 10110
www.wwnorton.com

W. W. Norton & Company Ltd., 10 Coptic Street, London WC1A 1PU

0 9 8 7 6 5 4 3 2 1

Contents

1
Introduction

Ordinary buildings resist easy definition as man-made objects. Even the most sophisticated are essentially handmade on site, even the most similar contain differences, even the most obvious contain hidden surprises. No one investigates a chair before purchase, but hiring a professional to inspect a house is accepted as a given. Unlike a chair, a house cannot be judged adequate on the basis of how it looks or how comfortable it is.

Any number of physical aspects of a building can be investigated, including architectural style, basic building structure, technical systems such as waterproofing, mechanical systems such as water supply, and the history of use. Structure and technical systems are investigated most frequently and are arguably the most important, since they determine the feasibility of changes in use and the expected lifespan of the building. The supporting structure of a building, and the method in which rain falling on the roof is transported to the ground, are not readily changed. By contrast, if the building structure is sound, mechanical systems are easily changed and are often modernized and upgraded when no other work is being performed.

The importance of investigation is directly related to the difficulty in changing the portion of a building under discussion, which can be described as the inherent lifespan of that portion. Structure, waterproofing systems, and window location and size, which are difficult to change, are investigated often and thoroughly, while usually only the most basic elements of mechanical systems are investigated with the alteration of minor portions (such as rerouting a duct) being assumed. Finally, a building's history may be very interesting but is not relevant except in cases where the history is the most important aspect of a building, such as with historic house museums.

The organization of this book follows the basic order of an investigation:

- identification of building type and systems
- identification and prioritizing of damage
- documentation of field conditions
- if the conditions warrant it, on-site probes and testing to further the investigation

Why Investigate Buildings?

Architects and engineers ordinarily learn investigation *ad hoc*, on the job. As a result, there has been little discussion of investigation theory and practice. It is obvious to anyone who has ever attempted to explain how to conduct investigations that there is more to the topic than a simple list of information to be found. Investigation is complicated because it ordinarily requires a good working knowledge of actual building construction, some familiarity with the appearance of deterioration of ordinary building materials and assemblies, and the ability to systematically examine and draw conclusions from incomplete information. The first two requirements demand more extensive building knowledge than is taught in college; the third requires organizational technique that is difficult to apply without such building knowledge.

This book explains what is ordinarily possible and how it is achieved. It intentionally avoids two extremes: small-scale reviews (such as those performed before shingle replacement on a wood-framed house), which are almost always performed either by the contractor carrying out ordinary maintenance work, or a specialized house investigator; and large-scale, minutely detailed investigations (such as those performed by architects before the historic restoration of a national monument or by an engineer as part of a forensic analysis of a collapse). The first is usually performed far too casually for the methods in this book; the second, though it uses most of the techniques and logic described here, requires specialized techniques and far more time and detail than is practical for ordinary purposes and typical, privately owned buildings.

The vast majority of investigations are in the middle ground between a casual look-over and a detailed analysis. Building owners and buyers, architects and engineers preparing for alterations, and contractors organizing their work require a systematic approach to learning the physical reality of a specific building. A useful approach consists of a number of discrete steps, all of which must be completed even if they are performed simultaneously or out of order. The steps include identification of the building type and systems, identification of damage, usable documentation of field conditions, and analysis of the findings in light of the investigation goal. Goals can vary from determining feasibility of alteration to determining liability for nonperformance of a building system.

How an investigation proceeds depends, in part, on the investigator. Structural engineers (like the author) look first for causes related to stiffness and force flow; materials conservationists study weathering patterns; architects search for evidence of previous alterations. All of these variables (and others) may be present simultaneously, but the order in which they are noted and the importance given to them may depend on the observer. Ideally, starting from any point will lead to the same conclusions, but it is still important that specialists performing investigations have sufficient knowledge of the other fields and know when additional expertise is required. Most thorough investigations are conducted by a team—an architect, a structural engineer, and a mechanical engineer are a standard group. The team for a complicated building may also include a conservationist, an expert in hazardous materials, and an elevator consultant. Smaller investigations are ordinarily conducted by a multidisciplined professional, often an architect, or have a narrow focus that can be covered by one of the people mentioned above.

Building Owners and Investigation

Owners, tenants, real-estate managers, and potential owners or tenants may request investigations and may perform them. The expertise of people in this group ranges from none, in the case of first-time home buyers, to professional-level training, as with building managers trained as architects. Owners or tenants who are not building professionals but are intimately familiar with a building can speed and improve the process of investigation if they add focus to problem finding. They may also hinder an investigation if their lack of technical knowledge prompts them to come to wrong conclusions early in the process. Nonprofessionals typically need a professional guide to interpret technical issues; a consultant who can explain what is seen or provide a thorough written explanation of the building type is essential.

Building Professionals and Investigation

Design professionals, as their name suggests, are concerned with the act of creation. Even when the subject of design is the alteration of, or an addition to, an existing building, it is the new construction aspect of the work that captures the imagination of most architects and engineers. As with any profession, there is specialization within architecture and engineering, and the wide field of alteration and the narrower one of conservation have drawn many architects who enjoy the challenge of adapting their design to an existing building.

Much of the logic and many of the techniques used in building investigation are the same as the logic and techniques used in new design, but employed in reverse. Instead of working to design the optimal column grid for a building or the best detail for support of a curtain wall, people investigating a building are measuring an existing column grid and trying to understand, from limited information, how a curtain wall is supported and waterproofed. This process can be described as a detective story; a few visual clues can reveal an idea that exists in built form but is not self-explanatory or documented.

Specialized training is needed to properly investigate some technical systems. The roof waterproofing methods and materials in an old building may be obsolete and therefore not discussed in an ordinary contemporary architectural education. For most architects, an education in the technology of old buildings comes on site, by working on the buildings in question under the direction of more experienced colleagues. Learning through direct experience is a valuable and flexible technique, as long as the professional has enough knowledge to know when he or she doesn't have enough knowledge to continue.

Engineers focus on current technique and future construction just as architects do. Current architectural space planning and design bear some resemblance to that taught in 1930, but technical issues may be entirely different, and engineering education is almost entirely concerned with technical issues. Historical and empirical analysis, which form the basis of the examination of existing buildings, are foreign to engineering education. Using modern codes and methods, engineers investigating new buildings can safely analyze structure, but the investigation of older buildings requires both the use of modern codes and standards and an understanding of the original design conditions and assumptions.

In building construction, structural engineering necessarily takes a subsidiary role to architecture. In civil works—bridges, dams, roads—the purpose of the structure is solely its proper functioning. An ugly structure may be less valued by its users and neighbors, but it performs as well as a beautiful structure. While architects often impart some aesthetic sense to civil projects, many structures considered to be landmarks, such as the Brooklyn Bridge or Hoover Dam, are not decorated per se, but simply emphasize the beauty of the structure.

Buildings represent an entirely different situation. No matter how important or innovative the structure of a building is, it is the architecture and, to a lesser degree, the mechanical engineering that determines how users perceive the building. Only the massing and facades affect the neighbors' opinions, and those aspects are ultimately under the control of the architect. A building where structure seems to determine the architecture, such as Chicago's John Hancock Building, could be kept structurally unchanged but given a new identity by adding cladding that cantilevers an additional inch or two further from the steel frame, and hides the cross-bracing.

Several types of work fall into the category of structural investigation: identification of structural type, examination of structural condition and capacity, and design of the interface between new structure and old. These are additions to engineers' ordinary responsibilities of structural design and review during construction, and are the structural counterparts to the architectural preservation work of identifying a building's original style and detail, researching its history, and designing alterations that fit its renovation or restoration.

Mechanical engineering investigation is often simpler than structural investigation because of the inherently shorter lifespan of the systems in question. For example, cooling towers are designed to be replaced after a period of time, so replacing them is far less involved than replacing structural elements such as columns, which are meant to last as long as the building stands. Compared with structural engineering, mechanical engineering is less focused on analyzing existing systems for reuse or adaptation and more focused on finding ways to integrate modern systems without disrupting historic material, ornate finishes, or existing tenants.

Engineering investigations of older buildings may be part of a historic preservation project, whether or not the building is officially considered to be a historic landmark. Historic preservation is often assumed to be of interest only to architects. Most literature and discussion on preservation concerns the finished (visible) surfaces of buildings, so it is easy for an engineer to get the impression that structural and mechanical work in preservation projects is no different from that in other renovation projects. This is not true. The architects and preservationists who are the prime consultants on preservation projects may have limited knowledge of structural and mechanical design and the history of structural materials and mechanical systems, leaving care of engineering preservation to the engineers. From the very beginning of the project, during investigation, it is the responsibility of engineers to find and explain these less common and less glamorous issues.

Engineering materials and design methods have changed greatly since the introduction of analysis-based rational design in the mid-nineteenth century. The "common sense" of an engineer trained only in current technique (for example, that buildings with iron columns and floor beams have a framing-connection-based lateral load system) may be totally wrong. Investigation can have dual purposes: to educate the designer about the specific building and to serve as a refresher course in the technology of a particular era. The greatest danger lies in making rapid assumptions based on incomplete or inaccurate knowledge. The ability to make an educated guess always requires education; conclusions, which are often educated guesses, should be the last step in an investigation, taken only after the engineer is familiar with the type of building being examined.

When engineers take part in historic preservation work, their control of the project is one step further removed than in ordinary practice: not only must they react to the dictates of the project architect, but they must also work within the set of constraints imposed by the philosophy of preservation. Engineers rarely know, let alone understand, these constraints, as they are often in conflict with the logic of engineering education and practice. Sustainable development has become a goal of progressive engineers, but this ideal is often stated in terms of the energy use and pollution of new construction, not in the sociological terms of saving cultural heritage and preserving pieces of the past that do not meet current standards of engineering design. For example, in most of Manhattan since the middle of the nineteenth century, it has been illegal to build a commercial building with wood-joist floors. But those that still exist and are in reparable condition have value (even when the wood is not visible) simply because these buildings represent a vanished past. This point escapes most engineers, even those performing renovations.

There is an additional concern when engineers not trained in preservation take part in the renovation of historic buildings. Unlike contemporary building materials, obsolete materials are not standardized, lack documentation, and, most important, behave unpredictably. For example, unreinforced masonry of unknown quality, including terra-cotta tile arch floors and partitions, makes up the bulk of most buildings built before 1900; cast iron was used for beams, where its unpredictable tensile strength affects every attempt at analysis. The reinforcing rods used in concrete construction before 1947 did not bond with the concrete as well as those of modern reinforcing, which means connection details require analysis that in a newer structure would be unnecessary. Attempting to alter such structures without understanding them usually leads to excessive replacement of old structure with modern, better-understood elements.

On-site Presence

Architects and engineers are most visible to the public and client during the design of a new building or alteration. Before construction there is no physical work to take attention away from the progress, on paper, of the design. Professionals have various duties after the design is reasonably complete and construction begins, most of which (e.g., shop-drawing review) are technical and do not require much client contact or generate much client interest. There are two stages when the architects and engineers may be on site regularly: during preliminary investigation as part of design, and to observe the work during construction. This book is concerned with investigation, but the two types of professional site work are linked.

Ordinary architects and engineers do not create or alter buildings, no matter how intimately connected to the construction process they may be. Rather, they create designs represented on paper, while the contractors create the physical building. The disconnection between the designer's intentions and what is happening on site is a constant concern for designers, who use site visits as a way to obtain firsthand information. Investigation site visits create familiarity with an existing building before the design of an alteration. Without a knowledge of the base conditions before design, site visits during alteration construction may be of little value.

The designers are not the only people visiting the site during construction. A professional may hear many conflicting stories from various people (other professionals, building owners, contractors, lawyers, insurance agents) who have an interest in both the quality of work and assigning blame for mistakes. The architect or engineer bearing responsibility for the design wants to visit the site during construction to obtain firsthand information, but the desire to obtain as much information as possible may conflict with the need to limit liability and with contractual definitions of the scope of the professionals' work. Pre-construction investigation is often free of these limitations.

One aspect of this question, legal responsibility for site safety, has been well investigated in theory and in various courts. A designer is not responsible for the safety of the contractor's operations on site unless the designer has explicitly taken on the job of site supervision or site-safety inspection. At the same time, if a designer becomes aware of an unsafe condition while on site, whether before or during construction, professional ethics and responsibility require that the people in control of the site be immediately informed.

Professionals want some degree of on-site presence during construction to protect themselves against honest contractors' mistakes and also, perhaps, less-than-honest misinterpretation. Investigation before design is unfortunately less common. Depending on the age of the building and the amount of documentation available, an entire design may be completed with minimal site investigation, with dimensions, beam sizes, and connection types marked for the contractor's benefit as "Verify in Field" or "Determine in Field."

If every project could be completed by making assumptions and adding verification notes in this manner, this study of investigation obviously would be unnecessary. In reality, few alteration projects can proceed without investigation of some type, and even fewer professionals are willing to go ahead with construction without investigating on-site conditions.

Repair versus Reconstruction

Investigation presupposes an existing building, which in turn indicates that alteration or reuse is being considered as an alternate to demolition and new construction. Taking the logic of retaining the existing structure one step further, one enters the contest between repairing as much existing material as possible and replacing individual building elements.

Alteration is typically a better solution than demolition and replacement because it usually is buildable, economical, and better suited to the conditions on site. The principles of historic preservation, as well as common sense, promote retaining as much original material as possible. Structures can stabilize in many unpredictable ways, using nondesigned load paths (for instance, masonry curtain walls may pick up load when steel beams are damaged) and residual strength provided by the difference between design strength and failure strength. While these "accidental" structural supports cannot be relied upon on a long-term basis, they are often quite stable until disturbed. Designs that take this stability into account and leave as much of the contributing material as possible realistically accept and use the actual conditions.

There are exceptions to the theory that retaining existing material is the best solution, which is why it cannot be stated more exactly than as a typical condition. The exceptions are usually caused by substandard existing material. A building under examination may turn out to have original design or construction flaws, severe weathering in inaccessible locations, or any combination of the three. In these cases, retaining the original structure may mean deliberately keeping building material that is effectively useless. Despite these exceptions, the goal of retaining original material should govern early thought on restoration and most renovations; this is the engineering version of one of the basic principles of historic preservation. Before 1970, few engineers had ever heard building problems defined in these terms; since then, there has been a gradual increase in sensitivity to the question, in response to the growing importance of architectural preservation.

One of the most important reasons for engineers to reuse material in place is that it saves energy embodied in existing materials and assemblies, effort in performing additional work (and in construction, effort equals money), and any potential historic fabric. Additionally, it helps avoid potential hazardous-material-disposal problems (e.g., lead paint on steel, coal clinker in cinder concrete, and asbestos fireproofing or roofing).

The nonengineering reasons for retaining original material are generally philosophical. These reasons, which are largely concerned with the history and cultural importance of the building, have been explored at great length elsewhere, primarily in preservation publications not read by many building owners, engineers, or contractors. Regardless of how desirable reuse may be, it cannot be seriously considered for either renovation or damage repair unless a thorough investigation of the existing structure has taken place. Little knowledge of an existing structure is needed to demolish it, but proper design of repairs requires fairly extensive information.

Historical Context

In order to fully understand a structure, it must be examined in context. For architects, proper context includes the time, place, societal influences, and stylistic background of the governing design theories. A medieval gothic building is a straightforward expression of the architectural design techniques and the best construction technology of the time; a building of the same style from the year 1890 would be an expression of an ideological belief that ignored the modern construction technology of that time. Engineers tend to ignore contextual issues, classifying them as "only architectural," but context affects the use of an analysis of historic design codes in the establishment of the method and boundaries of the original design.

For example, consider the use of iron. Wrought-iron beams were used with cast-iron columns by the engineers and constructors of the mid-nineteenth century because cast iron was the strongest material for direct compression they knew of and wrought iron, which could withstand compression and tension equally well, was ideally suited to bending. Engineers no longer use cast-iron columns for two reasons. First, modern theory has shown that ductility is more important than gross compressive capacity, and second, the development of the skeleton frame demands columns capable of withstanding substantial bending in addition to compression. This change is the result of advances in theory and metalworking capability, but it does not represent a new way of seeing buildings as much as it is a continuation of the scientific methods of engineering design that first developed in the mid-nineteenth century. An understanding of the context (in this case, the development of structural-analysis methods) simplifies the on-site investigation by providing an expected finding. It is the "education" in an educated guess.

We are not inherently smarter or better designers than our predecessors; if, when examining their designs, we fail to understand their motives, we are essentially being less smart and less competent than they were. All investigations should start with the idea that there was a reason for everything that was done in the past. The architectural reasons tend to trace back to the governing design theories, either in application or in reaction. The engineering reasons are the same as those that govern now: efficient design, economic use of material, site logistics, and other buildability constraints.

Definitions

This book is geared toward architects and engineers, who are technical professionals with specialized training and who tend to use specialized language. While the methods and concepts discussed are those of technical investigation, nontechnical language is used as much as possible, because it better illustrates the points.

Specialized language often can be avoided, with some exceptions. A few terms that are useful in describing the topics of interest but are not part of the experience of the average person are defined here.

- "Field" and "on site" are used interchangeably to describe work performed in or around the building in question. Research in an archive, although performed outside of the investigator's office, is not fieldwork; walking around the perimeter of the building and taking pictures with a disposable camera to document the conditions on a specific day, is.
- An "element" is an individual piece of construction. An element may be made of other elements, so the use of the word depends on the context. When you are discussing a facade, windows and piers are elements; when you are discussing windows and piers, individual mullions and bricks are elements.
- A "member" is an individual major structural element. A beam, a joist, a column, or a single span of floor slab may be described as a member, but a bolt cannot be.
- A "mechanism" is a physical explanation of events. When something occurs (e.g., damage to members, building movement, or even simply support of gravity loads), there must be a reasonable (and above all else practical) explanation. The physical representation of that explanation

is a mechanism. Freeze-thaw cycles are a mechanism that heaves sidewalks; sidesway is a mechanism that cracks partitions in tall buildings; mullion deflection is a mechanism that causes glass in glass curtain walls to crack. Note that each of these is "a mechanism," not "the mechanism." There are often several possible mechanisms that can individually or collectively explain the situation. Part of investigation is determining the mechanism or mechanisms responsible for any damage noted.

2
Investigation
Principles

Despite the enormous variety of building types, sizes, and conditions, a relatively small number of principles come into play during an investigation. These principles may be expressed in many different ways, depending on the building in question, but are unchangeable and govern anything from the investigation of the construction of gothic cathedrals to the exploration of modern office buildings or spec-built private houses.

The principles can be divided into two broad groups: those that relate to the physical nature of buildings and those that relate to the investigators. Ways to discuss various physical aspects of investigation include:

- identifying types of building systems
- looking for evidence of movement at the structural-member or building-wide scale
- looking for evidence of material deterioration from weathering
- identifying the loads present
- identifying combinations of movement, deterioration, and load effects

Following are six ways in which an investigator can approach the physical aspects of investigation:

- making sure all aspects have been addressed
- identifying places from which a building can be observed
- identifying ways in which information may be hidden from observation
- making educated guesses about unknown information
- learning the ways in which drawings show reality
- learning the ways in which construction differs from design

Not all of the principles will come into play in every investigation, but they all are potentially important and apply to all types of buildings under all conditions.

The examples given with each principle are common in existing buildings. Not coincidentally, most of them are forms of damage. In an undamaged, ordinary building, the construction is hidden beneath architectural finishes. Only when the finished surfaces are damaged does the structure become visible, either through its effect on the finishes or through gaps in the finish envelope. The examples given with each principle are just a few of the many types of damage that can be found.

Identification

One of the most fundamental reasons to conduct an investigation is to identify the basics of the building systems for future planning and design purposes. Architectural style is the easiest item to identify. Since the style is meant to be visible, a walk-through of a building and its site usually provides enough information for a novice to look up the style in a handbook. Since this information is literally superficial—concerned with the appearance and layout of the building—it does not directly help determine the details of construction. However, an examination of the condition of the finished surfaces is useful in structural identification.

As described in the section on interaction of building elements, many construction details can be deduced from minor damage to finished surfaces. This relationship between finish appearance and structure works both ways: the severity of damage implied by the visible evidence depends on the type of structure being examined just as the type of structure may be revealed by damage. Identifying the structural type must be an early goal if you want to make logical inferences about the information gathered during the investigation.

The early stages of an investigation consist almost entirely of gathering information, either on site or from available records. This is a good time for the investigator to make an educated guess about the structural type (e.g., wood-joist floors supported on brick bearing walls for a rowhouse), or possibly several guesses if the evidence gathered up to that point is ambiguous. Having an assumed type helps to focus the field effort and provides a framework within which assumptions about structural member locations and sizes are proved or disproved and replaced with assumptions based on better-documented facts.

The identification of mechanical systems requires a combination of direct and inferential techniques. Portions of the systems are exposed to view, allowing for direct identification, while inferences must be made about the hidden portions. Investigation of mechanical systems is usually conducted simultaneously with architectural investigation, making the identification phase a good time to coordinate findings about the visible portions of the building.

Building Movement

Every building moves, and every building decays. Furthermore, every element in a building moves and every material decays. The amount of movement may be too small to notice and the amount of decay may be too small to cause visible damage, but both are always present. These two facts are at the core of any building investigation. The effects of movement and decay are usually related and always mixed together, so that finding the cause of a known problem or discovering basic facts about a building means deciphering the particular building's dynamics. This section discusses the causes and effects of movement; the following section, the causes and effects of decay.

The science of mechanics of materials defines the relationship between the forces acting on an object and the resulting deformation of that object. While the details of this relationship are a technical design issue for structural engineers, the effects are visible to anyone who has ever seen a sagging floor or cracks in the plaster on a stud wall. For any given structure, it is possible to predict movements based on the strength and stiffness of the designed structural elements. However, nonstructural elements—that is, pieces of the building that were not intended or designed to carry load—may carry load, which sometimes makes the models used to determine deflection inaccurate, oversimplified, or incomplete. In addition, since the loads used in design represent probabilistic maximum loads and not those ordinarily seen in actual use, real-life deflections tend to be less than those predicted. The simpler a structure is, the more accurately deflection under load can be determined. In the complex systems of complete buildings, the motion of individual pieces of the building and the paths through which load travels between those pieces may be different than those intended by the buildings' designers. If the discrepancies are small, they may be unimportant. If large, they will lead to the damage and serviceability defects that initiate building investigations.

For the investigator, the most important effect of structural movement is differential stiffness. Beams of different sizes have different stiffnesses—that is, they move in different amounts even when loaded similarly—but the differences are relatively small, with beams in close proximity usually being within thirty to fifty percent of each other's stiffness. Different types of structural elements in close proximity can have enormously different stiffnesses: a beam carrying the weight of a wall may be less than a hundredth of the stiffness of the wall, and a wall loaded in plane may be more than a thousand times stiffer than the same wall loaded out of plane. As a result, when different structural elements move under load, joints between elements that were flush and tight open up and become visible. Examples of differential stiffness are damage to interior partitions in high-rises that have large amounts of sidesway when subjected to lateral load from wind or earthquake forces, crushing at the tops of interior partitions and the floors above them as the floors move under gravity load, and cracking where interior beams meet masonry facades. (Figure 2-1)

In the same way that different configurations of structure have different stiffnesses, different materials have inherently different properties, including Young's modulus, the common measurement of inherent stiffness. As a result, structural elements that have similar configurations but are made of different materials will have similar geometric stiffnesses but different material stiffnesses. The same types of damage described above for geometric stiffness may affect different materials forced into contact, such as concrete block and brick within a wall, steel columns and surrounding brick piers, or glass panels in curtain walls and the adjacent metal frames.

Because most investigations are performed on buildings that have most or all of their interior and exterior finishes intact, direct observation of structure is often difficult. As a result, building investigations performed by visual examination focus on secondary effects, such as measurable

2-1. In a building already identified as having a reinforced concrete frame, the wall behind the storage shelves is a concrete block partition. The partition does not carry structural load, so the cracking where the block meets the concrete is not serious. It is probably the result of minor frame movements, shrinkage of the mortar used to place the block, and out-of-plane impact within this room and the one on the opposite side of the partition.

deflections of structure, or tertiary effects, such as deflection or damage to finishes, rather than on primary effects, such as stress within the structure. Testing, whether destructive or nondestructive, is the only way to get a real idea of stress: almost all mechanical or electronic monitoring methods reveal deflection rather than actual stress.

To identify movement as a cause of damage requires some engineering knowledge, but an examination of the effects does not. It is possible to identify patterns of damage and to surmise that they may be linked to structural movement, but a thorough engineering examination requires that a rational series of questions regarding the movement be posed. Even if the investigator lacks the technical knowledge to analyze the answers to these questions, asking and answering them will help categorize damage as severe or not severe. In general, the more complicated the patterns of damage, the more basic the structural cause—for example, the lack of a proper lateral load system may cause complicated cracking in facades.

- Is the damage worse at the top of the building than at the bottom?
- Worse at the bottom than at the top?
- Are cracks diagonal, vertical, horizontal, or a combination of directions?
- Is the damage located primarily on one face of the building, on opposing faces, or on adjacent faces?
- Does the damage appear to be active (ongoing) at the time of the investigation or does it seem to have taken place in the past? Are the edges of cracks sharp (new) or rounded (old)?
- Have cracks widened, indicating movement in one direction, or do they seem to be working back and forth (opening and closing over time)?
- What is the load history of the building?
- What are the local conditions outside of the building (microclimate); are there neighboring buildings?
- Has the arrangement of neighboring buildings changed?
- Do exposures face water or open land?
- Have there been changes in the microclimate?

When you are looking at movement in buildings, keep in mind the simple but counterintuitive fact that there is no such thing as a truly nonstructural element. Every portion of a building (including secondary metal framing, modern curtain-wall elements, masonry curtain-wall elements, semibearing masonry, attachments for mechanical systems, and difficult-to-categorize elements such as loose steel lintels) carry structural loads: those of their own weight and other weights, direct wind, direct seismic, and secondary stresses. Buildings with wood-joist floors, wood subfloor, and black-iron ceiling hangers have been known to carry structural loads when the joists were damaged. Other examples of nonstructural elements carrying structural load include stud partitions in reinforced concrete frames, which are often stiffer than the floor slabs, and masonry curtain walls on high-rise steel-frame buildings. Since all elements carry some form of load, all will move to some degree.

A good example of simple building movement can be found in the "jack arch" window heads that older brick-wall buildings often have instead of angle lintels. Jack arches are shallow arches constructed of two to three courses of common brick set within the flat field of brick around the window. They were favored for rear-facade windows during the nineteenth century and as late as the 1940s because they were simple for masons to create while building the wall. Jack arches, as usually built, are not very strong. The brick used for the arch is an ordinary size and shape with thick, wedge-shaped joints, rather than the brick having the wedge shape that should be used for arches. The jack arch's two or three simple courses of brick do not create adequate bearing at the arch ends. Varying stresses within the wall often cause what is called a three-point failure, where cracks begin at the bottom center of the arch and at the top of the arch at its ends. (Figure 2-2) In extreme cases, the end cracks will extend up to the window sill above. This damage is directly attributable to the difference in stiffness and strength of the arch and the wall as a whole.

Another simple example is damage to the parapets in large warehouse

2-2. Failure of a brick jack arch window head.

buildings with uninsulated steel-deck roofs. When subjected to extremes in temperature (from a hot, sunny day to a cold, overcast day) the roof structure will grow and shrink as much as an inch. If the connection of the roof to the parapets at its edge does not allow for this movement, the parapets will be subjected to an outward thrust every time the roof grows in the heat. It is not unusual to find the parapets on a building of this type cracked and leaning outward.

A more complicated example is when interior partitions inadvertently carry load as if they were bearing walls. When the nonbearing partitions in a wood building are erected, they run from the top of the joists of one floor to the bottom of the joists of the next. When the floor above is loaded, the joists deflect downward, just like any other beam. In joist buildings, however, the difference between a load-bearing wall and a mere partition may be small or even nonexistent: interior bearing walls and nonbearing partitions in houses will both be built of two-by-four studs with two-by-four sole and top plates. When the joists deflect they may come to rest on partitions near the middle of the span, which will then begin to carry load. Because the partitions may not have the support required to carry the load, the plaster below or on the sides of the partitions often cracks. Ordinarily, this is not dangerous because the walls that were meant to carry load are present and will pick up the load as the partitions gradually crack and settle, but the presence of the cracks is alarming to anyone who has not identified the mechanism at work.

Material Deterioration

Regardless of the claims made by manufacturers and users of "miracle products," every material decays. More precisely, the physical properties of materials change over time as the materials are exposed to various chemical reactions (hydration and acid attack from rainwater), external energy sources (ultraviolet radiation from sunlight), and mechanical action (thermal expansion and contraction). The changes vary from minor mechanical breakdown to chemical alterations of the physical properties of the material. Minor mechanical breakdown, such as the denting of metal flashing from the impact of roof gravel moved by high winds, does not usually cause problems elsewhere in the building. An extreme example of chemical changes, such as the rusting of steel beams, could cause collapse.

A common example of deterioration is the water damage found in

2-3. Removal of the plank floor and plaster inside an 1840s rowhouse shows severe water damage to the brick below the window as well as damage to the joists in this area, a bathroom.

buildings with wood-joist floors. In both private houses and multistory, wood-joist apartment houses, water damage can usually be found in the kitchens and bathrooms. (Figure 2-3) This might seem obvious, but it is actually the result of four separate damage-causing mechanisms. First, water that is on the floor, either from sloppiness during use of the fixtures or from cleaning, will eventually seep through the tile or other protective floor covering. Second, the plumbing hidden within the floor and partitions may have slow leaks that never release enough water to cause a visible problem but do release a steady supply of water into the floor. Third, plumbing that does not leak often "sweats" from condensation, again creating a supply of water within the floor structure. Fourth, every drain has a vent stack that rises through the building until it passes through the roof. The flashing at the vents creates weak points in the roofing that are far more likely to leak than the roof membrane as a whole.

One of the most common and easy-to-find forms of damage is the effect of water entry through the walls of a steel-frame building. No facade system is perfectly waterproof, and small leaks over time cause gradual rusting of the outside faces of the columns and beams making up

2-4. The brick piers of this concrete-frame building have bulges and horizontal cracks at numerous locations—in this picture, left and right of center and at the upper left—but always in the same place locally. All of the bulges and cracks are near the mid-point of a floor and run straight across the piers. Such a regular pattern suggests a design phenomenon rather than weathering.

2-5. The cracks in the side of the brick pier are all oriented the same way, diagonally from the building side at the top to the outboard side at the bottom. This pattern is consistent with movement outward and up, which runs counter to the assumption that loose masonry tends to fall.

Investigation Principles

2-6. Cutting a probe at a bulge and crack shows a steel shelf angle for brick support, badly rusted at both legs. Rust in the vertical leg has pushed the angle away from the concrete column, creating the bulge. Rust in the horizontal leg has jacked up the brick, creating the crack

the frame of the building. Rust occupies more space than steel, so as the steel rusts, it expands and gradually pushes out the nearby facade elements. This in turn usually causes cracks or gaps that allow more water to enter, accelerating the rusting. Visible cracks or bulges in a facade often indicate the invisible presence of rust on the beams or columns. (Figures 2-4, 2-5, 2-6)

Load Types

There is a direct correlation between the type of loads a portion of a building was designed to carry and the physical form of the member. A member meant to carry compression (columns and bearing walls) tends to be stocky and may be made of a material (e.g., masonry) that cannot easily carry tension or bending. Pure tension members are rare in buildings and, since they are usually made of steel, are often indistinguishable from small columns. However, small amounts of tension may be carried by simple steel rods, which are identifiable as tension members for the simple reason that they cannot carry any other form of load.

The third possible form of load, bending, may be the most difficult to identify directly, but structural logic often will make the case. A member spanning horizontally and loaded from above carries gravity loads between its supports and will therefore be in bending. A member spanning vertically at the exterior of a building carries wind load to the building as a whole and is in bending. There are other types of bending members, but these two are the most common.

In buildings that have structural systems composed of more than one material, the material used for a given element may identify the type of load expected in design for that element. Unreinforced masonry piers can only carry compressive load and are used in conjunction with wood or steel beams and joists. In a building with these elements, you can safely assume that the wood and steel are carrying bending and the masonry is carrying compression. Wood and steel shapes are capable of carrying compression, tension, and bending; reinforced concrete is used for bending and compression; unreinforced concrete and masonry are used for compression; and steel rods and cables can only carry tension.

Interaction of Building Elements

The effect of differential stiffness described in the section on building movement is a form of interaction. Interaction is defined here as the effect of two adjoining building elements that differ in at least one of these major characteristics: stiffness, thermal expansion, weathering characteristics, or strength. When combinations of different elements are subjected to varying conditions (changes in load, temperature, humidity, or material properties over time), interaction may be the best framework for understanding any damage present. This happens most frequently on building facades, where different elements are combined in locations subject to varying weather conditions. The effects of interaction are usually the combined effects of overstress, movement, and material deterioration.

Differences in thermal characteristics between materials in contact often cause interaction damage. For example, buildings that have portions of a concrete frame exposed on the outside for architectural purposes undergo differential thermal movement. The exposed portions of the concrete expand and contract with temperature changes, while the remainder of the concrete frame on the interior of the building, which is maintained at a roughly constant temperature, stays the same size. Interior partitions running perpendicular to the exterior walls can suffer damage from the movement as their outside ends move up and down while their inside ends stay still.

Another example of interaction is the presence of accidental stiffness in facade elements. Each piece of a facade (lintels, wall piers, flat wall areas, adjacent floor structure, adjacent structural columns) is designed individually for its dominant loads. The dominant loads on a typical loose lintel are the weight of a triangular section of wall directly above and the load from any floor structure directly above that is carried by the wall. The lintel is strong enough to carry these loads, but as a relatively small piece of steel, it is much less stiff than the weaker masonry it supports. Often the masonry supports itself when the wall is first built and then gradually eases onto the lintel as the mortar ages and the strength of the masonry decreases. This type of structural damage is not cause for concern—in fact, the elements of the building are simply starting to perform in the way they were designed—but it can cause cracking in the masonry joints above the lintel.

A final example of a complex interaction between building elements is damage to brick parapets on steel-frame buildings. Even when every element has been properly designed, the combinations may not work well. Through-wall flashing in the parapet (necessary for proper waterproofing) allows the parapet to move (rocking in and out of the wall plane) more than a plain masonry parapet would. This movement causes microscopic cracks in the mortar joints, into which water seeps. The base of the parapet therefore ages faster than the top, allowing more water into the brick face. Top-floor windows with loose lintels or hung lintels supporting the brick at the top floor may rust faster than similar steel elements further down the facade, and as they rust, their expansion forces the front of the parapet upward, exacerbating the problems. (Figure 2-7) No one element is failing, but the combined system has developed a problem.

Thoroughness

Any investigation must be complete if it is to make sense. The definition of "thoroughness" varies with the type of investigation: even a cursory inspection that only confirms that there is no major damage must be thorough in that it must include all areas of the building. The more complete the investigation, the more detailed it will be. A conditions survey (for example, a due-diligence examination before purchase) not only requires

2-7. Severe cracking in a facade's face brick caused by rusting of loose steel lintels over the windows. The entire portion of the facade above the top floor window heads, including the face of the parapets, has been lifted by rust jacking.

all areas of the building to be examined, but also requires examination of all major elements such as structure and building envelope.

While some "signature" buildings are composed entirely of unique spaces and therefore have greatly varying architectural, structural, and mechanical conditions, most buildings have extensive repetition of elements. Identification of the patterns of repetition, even if their meanings are not necessarily clear, should be performed early in the investigation, as part of establishing the type of construction. Once the basic patterns of the buildings are known, it is relatively easy to find exceptions. A systematic search for exceptions ensures the investigator's thoroughness: if the same exception is found repeatedly, it is obviously part of the pattern. A good example is found in the window layouts of tall buildings with masonry facades. If a vertical row of windows (the base pattern) is missing a window at one floor or has a double-width at one floor, this is excellent evidence of previous alterations.

When drawings of a building are not available before an investigation, the investigator must decide if drawings are needed. If the purpose of the investigation is to simply identify problems or perform a due-diligence check before purchase, a written report is usually enough. If the investigation is the first step toward repairing damage or making alterations, then drawings will be needed eventually, and the investigation must include on-site measurements. There are many inherent inaccuracies in measuring a building, but careful and repeated measurement followed by thorough documentation can produce a set of field-condition drawings good enough for any practical purpose. The most thorough examples of existing-conditions drawings are those created under the auspices of the Historic American Building Survey and the Historic American Engineering Record (HABS/HAER). These drawings provide complete architectural and engineering details of the known information. The level of field examination and the documentation that are required for HABS/HAER are not required for ordinary construction and condition assessment and are not economic for ordinary building owners looking for answers to a given question.

Being thorough often requires nothing more than patience. A simple example of a thorough examination is locating the source of a leak. Water can travel long distances inside buildings, both horizontally and vertically. While the majority of plumbing and roofing leaks show as damage to finishes near the problem, it is possible that you will not find a source of water when you open up a damaged plaster ceiling. Until a definite source can be identified, the search must continue, otherwise any effort spent in repairing the plaster will be wasted.

Useful Views

Because buildings are complex three-dimensional objects, even simple visual observation requires planning and organization. In the same way that a complete set of architectural drawings for a new building documents every surface (including those that may not be obvious, such as the interior of an exterior wall above a vestibule), complete investigation of a finished building includes observation of every surface. The locations for observation affect the building's image, and therefore should be carefully chosen.

The following list contains views that are usually obtainable during an investigation and that may provide useful information:

- information visible from the roof
- information visible from the surrounding streets and grounds
- information visible from neighboring roofs

2-8. A steel beam nearly buried in loose cinder fill. Probing has shown the bottom flange of the beam to be nearly 2 feet below the roofing membrane at the top of the picture.

- information visible from mid-air
- information visible within exterior rooms
- information visible in public halls
- information visible within interior rooms

From the roof

Many buildings have more than one roof level. Assuming that one or more roofs are accessible, they provide views of the roof itself, the inside faces of any parapets or exterior wall chimneys, and the outside faces of any bulkheads or penthouses. (Figure 2-8) In tall buildings, one of the most important views from a roof is the view down the face of the walls, which clearly shows out-of-plumb conditions and bulges. The most important piece of information that can be obtained while on flat roof is the quality of drainage.

From the surrounding streets and grounds

Buildings can stand entirely isolated, surrounded by other buildings on three sides, or with some adjacent construction and some adjacent yards.

By viewing the building from all available sides, complete examination of the lower portions of the exposed wall surfaces is possible. (Figures 2-9, 2-10)

2-9. A 1920s office building with a facade of stone panel veneer over brick back-up. From the street, no problems are visible; see Figure 2-11 for a closer view.

2-10. No severe damage is visible, but the heavy staining of the brick and the peeling paint on the sheet-metal cornice suggest that exterior maintenance has been minimal or nonexistent for some time.

From neighboring roofs

Buildings in cities are often difficult to examine. Other buildings obstruct the views, and views from the street yield little useful information concerning the top of the building. Examination of the building from the roofs of adjacent buildings can provide views of the walls and roof not otherwise obtainable. Of course, this type of examination requires cooperation from the neighbors.

From mid-air

A specialized form of investigation—facade examination of a tall building—requires specialized tools. Hanging scaffolding, which provides "hands-on" examination of the facades, is far more expensive than the simple technique of viewing the building from its surroundings, but it provides far more information. (Figure 2-11)

Within exterior rooms

Many of the potential problems with a building concern its exterior envelope. Evidence of waterproofing failures in the exterior walls or roofs and

2-11. A close-up view of Figure 2-9, taken from scaffolding, reveals a pattern of small patches to the stone, strongly suggesting that the veneer has been pinned back to the stone in the past, presumably as a repair of local failure.

excessive movement of lightly built exterior walls from wind motion can be found in the exterior spaces. Items that can be checked while standing in an exterior room include the joints between interior walls or partitions and the inside face of the exterior walls, the joints between the ceiling and the inside face of the exterior walls, and the inside surface of the exterior walls, particularly above and below windows.

In public halls

The public halls of multistory buildings are of interest for two reasons: as portions of the fire egress they are often designed for heavier live loads than the surrounding floors, and they abut the stair and elevator shafts. The first item means that the floors of the public halls may be of a heavier build than the other floors; the second means that there is a large change in stiffness where the floor meets the shafts. Both items create interaction conditions and may therefore be responsible for damage or exposed structure. The joints between the hall ceiling and the outside face of elevator and stair shaft walls should be examined, as should the juncture of the hall floor and ceiling with the adjacent interior space floor and ceiling.

Within interior rooms

In an ordinary room, it is difficult to obtain information about the hidden portions of the building. The living room of a home or an interior office is a finished space with little interaction damage and few effects from neighboring structure or systems. Such spaces must be examined when there is a known history of problems (e.g., a leak that is not below any known plumbing may indicate that there is a riser offset within the floor above), but usually only a representative sample of ordinary rooms need be included in an investigation.

Hidden Information

Except in rare cases when an old building is stripped down to its bare structural elements, a certain amount of guesswork must go into determining structure based on the evidence it leaves on the surrounding finishes. (Figure 2-12) Structural investigation often involves noting minor cracks or deflections that have no particular meaning until the surrounding rooms have been examined, when those cracks and deflections can be put in context. A common form of damage in wood-joist, masonry-bear-

2-12. A cast-iron column top at a pressed-tin ceiling. The identical seat connection lugs visible do not give a good indication as to the floor structure hidden above the tin.

ing-wall buildings is cracking where partitions meet exterior walls. These cracks often start at the partition-to-wall joint, near the ceiling, and spread down toward the floor and across the partition-to-ceiling joint away from the wall. They are most often the simple result of the stiffness of an eight-foot-deep diaphragm made of lath and plaster relative to the flexibility of the actual load-carrying floor joists. The joists move under load more than the partitions do, but since the partitions are incapable of carrying any load, they must dip with the floor, and there is differential movement at the joist-to-partition joints. The exterior wall moves least of all, and rarely out-of-plane. As the partition moves, it pulls away from this wall at its top and bottom corners, but baseboard moldings typically hide the motion at the bottom. The brittle plaster cracks, creating the illusion of a structural flaw. The reality is that the nonstructural partition is doing too much structurally: if it moved more under load, the cracks would be smaller. This example is one of the simplest cases of "hidden meaning" in structural examination. If only the cracks at the partition edges are seen, no conclusion can be drawn, but when the exterior wall is seen to be undamaged, and no signs of increasing movement of the floors or damage to the joists are observed, the context of the cracks clarifies their meaning.

Intuition

In a basic sense, intuition plays no role in investigation: a building is a physical object with properties that can be determined. However, intuition comes into play when a person with experience in design or on similar investigations cuts short much of the basic work. This applies to any design project: an experienced architect can make educated assumptions about how to begin a new project, and an experienced engineer can examine a set of architectural plans and make educated assumptions about the best form of structural or mechanical system. (Figure 2-13)

Based on the information derived from experience or from documentation, an investigator may have a "feeling" as to hidden conditions. Such educated guesses can serve as starting points, with standard investigative techniques used to confirm the assumptions. However, educated guesses are still guesses and cannot serve as anything more than a guide.

Practical Reality versus Graphics and the Theory of Drawing

Any form of architectural or engineering design is a theoretical representation of the world, a virtual reality described by drawings, computer

2-13. The extreme thickness of the exterior walls of this building, combined with the late-nineteenth-century date suggested by the architectural style, are strong evidence that this is a bearing-wall building. The arched openings on the left appear to be original, while the flat-top garage entrance on the right is almost certainly an alteration.

geometry, models, and retouched photographs. Each design profession has its own method of representing reality (with varying degrees of accuracy) but none is capable of or pretends to be capable of integrating all of a building in a set of construction drawings. All design professionals learn to be slightly wary of drawings not produced by themselves, particularly those produced by someone of a different discipline, whose view of reality as represented in their drawings may differ substantially and without warning from the reader's. Even as basic a fact as which floor is being represented can vary, as architects show the second floor on the second-floor plan, mechanical engineers show the ceiling of the second story (the underside of the third floor) on the second-floor plan, and structural engineers usually show the second-floor framing on the second-floor plan (except in house construction).

Investigation takes hold of the issue from the other end: instead of drafting a theoretical construct meant as the basis for actual construction, the investigator begins with the actual object and reduces it to a set of notes, drawings, and photographs. Even when the investigation includes original drawings, their representation of reality always takes second place to the real physical structure. Depending on the form of the original documentation, its value may vary widely, while the value of the actual investigation of the building never falls.

One of the most important differences between representation and reality is in the interaction of different building elements. The representation (as shown in detail drawings) implies that the interaction is limited and controlled—for example, a steel shelf angle supports the veneer brick in a curtain wall and is, in turn, supported by the cantilevered edge of the concrete flat slab, with no other possible interpretations. This view of the work is reinforced by theory (here, that curtain walls are incapable of carrying structural load) and by detailing practice (the wedge anchors that connect the shelf angles to the concrete can only take load downward). In actual construction, elements subjected to actual loads behave in ways theory doesn't acknowledge and interact across discipline lines. Elements that are not detailed on the same drawings (such as the concrete of the structural frame and the brick curtain wall) affect one another. Insufficient expansion joints in the curtain wall, creep of the frame concrete, and dimensional changes caused by varying loads can reduce the building's ability to accept movements caused by thermal changes and frame sidesway without the wall carrying vertical loads. Even if this effect does not involve high levels of stress and is intermittent, it may be a contributing cause to damage. When field observation uncovers cracking or bulging in a facade, the cause may be frame motion, in contradiction to the design and drawing theory that says stresses in curtain walls and structural frames are independent.

Just as documentary information can be obtained from unlikely sources (for example, duct shop drawings made from the mechanical design drawings, which were made from wash-offs of architectural reflected ceiling plans and therefore contain structural information, such as beam soffit locations), physical structural information can be obtained from non-structural elements. Gross movements show up in the condition of gypsum board, gypsum block, and terra-cotta partitions; plumbing runs can indicate the direction of framing or the presence of holes through structural members.

There are two useful sources of information: the actual structure, which corresponds to a primary source in academic research, and existing documentation, which corresponds to a secondary source. The best source of information is always the building itself. The most complete set of construction documents imaginable from conscientious engineers and architects do not necessarily reflect the exact built conditions; the built conditions themselves do. In addition, examination of the actual building may reveal deterioration or damage. Secondary sources of information, ranging from the hypothetical complete set of construction documents to partial drawings of other renovations, show someone's idea, or model, of existing conditions. That model must be tested by examination of the primary source, that is, by selective examination of the actual conditions the drawings represent. Interviewing someone familiar with the building's documentation or history, the equivalent of tertiary sources, should be done sparingly, if at all. Memory is too variable to be trusted when people's lives may be at risk. Talking with building superintendents, occupants, contractors, or even the building's designers can be useful as a starting point for an investigation, but without exception, every fact that comes from interviews has to be checked.

Architectural Design versus Building Construction

In a critique of the architecture of a building, certain principles come into play: the reviewer examines three-dimensional space, sequences of movement through the building, color, texture, symbolic use of ornament, hierarchy of spaces, and so on. During investigation, most of these principles do not advance understanding of the basic construction of the building. Details that are secondary in architectural thought, such as how a drain leader makes its way from a flat roof down to the main building drain to a sewer, usually bear no relation to the architectural meaning of the spaces traversed. It is possible for every element in a given building or space to be architecturally designed and significant, but the more complicated the building, the less likely this is. The economics of construction dictate that ordinary buildings are assemblages of ordinary elements, not of elements specifically designed for a given building. The frequency of special design varies depending on the element—so that light fixtures that are unique to a given building are relatively common (although present in well under half of all new buildings), unique exposed mechanical systems are rare, and unique structural elements rarest of all.

On the other hand, architectural significance cannot be ignored: the most complicated structure in steel-framed buildings is often involved with major public rooms. Large spaces at the base of a building require column transfers, long-span roofs, and other structure commensurate with the architectural importance. Also, minor damage that might be acceptable in a secondary space may be a crisis in a major room. So, while the intention of the designing architect may not be of interest during an investigation, the results of those intentions are present in the physical artifact. Written descriptions of the architectural theory or the design intent may be useful—at least as guides to the architectural meaning of the building if not to the actual details of construction.

3
Building
Types

Every building is unique, because every one is assembled by hand from basic components (even if those components are as large as a two-story section of prefabricated curtain wall). Multiple buildings constructed from one set of plans will be slightly different; buildings with similar appearances and layouts constructed at different times may be wildly different. The existence of these differences is, of course, the base cause of investigation.

Architectural history and discussions of architectural style tend to concentrate on showpiece buildings, even when those buildings are showpieces of a common style or a typical building system. The vast majority of buildings are relatively ordinary and can be classified by their use, their structure, and their architectural style (whether conscious or unconscious on the part of the designers and builders). Structural type is the most critical classification, as it determines the feasibility of changes and suggests damage that may be present even if it is not visible. An investigator examining a building of unknown construction will identify material and geometric features and use them to classify the building. Obviously, some features have more meaning than others: concrete columns almost always indicate a reinforced concrete frame (no other ordinary structural system uses concrete columns), while a wood plank floor means relatively little, as it could be either the actual floor over wood joists or simply an architectural finish over any other type of floor.

Any discussion of "types" assumes that there is an underlying organization—that the features of interest form patterns can be found and labeled. The standard features described below include:

- exterior wall types (architectural/structural)
- roof types (architectural)
- masonry structure types
- wood structure types
- steel structure types
- concrete structure types

Standard Building Types

As described in the section on identifiable structural features, certain portions of a structure are more visible than others. There are recognizable standard types for certain building systems: the basic structural frame (related to age, size, use, local materials, and fire codes), the type of floors (related to age, use, local materials, and fire codes), the type of exterior walls (related to age, use, and architectural style), and the various mechanical systems.

If every building examination began from scratch, and relied solely on the strength of the examiner's observation, investigation would be very difficult. This difficulty arises on occasion, but it is rare because most buildings fall into one of a limited number of types. If investigation can establish the building type, an educated guess about unseen details can be made, and later checked. In short, investigation can be seen as simultaneously establishing two separate facts: the class to which the building belongs, and details concerning the specific building. The importance of any observed fact depends on the type of building, so conclusions about a building element or damage cannot be made until the type is determined.

Mechanical systems have shorter life spans than the basic structural systems, and they are more easily changed if they are damaged, obsolete, or inadequate for changing occupancy. Structural systems, which are not changeable without massive reconstruction of a building and which have life spans more or less identical to their buildings, are used for identifying types.

Standard building types vary from one locality to another and with time. The standards for load capacity, materials, and design techniques for a given location are different at different dates, and the types for a given time vary from one location to another. Standard structural types develop for a number of reasons. A material may be easily obtained and therefore inexpensive—for example, the availability of lumber from forests in the South and the upper Midwest has driven the use of wood for private houses in the eastern half and the western seaboard of the United States. A locally popular architectural style may be well suited to a specific system—for example, the architectural desire for the skyscraper led to the rapid development of steel-framing designs in Chicago and New York between 1890 and 1930. As specific architectural styles come in and out of fashion, they may change the requirements for structural systems; steel or concrete frames in buildings of all uses and sizes accommodated the enormous popularity of the International style in the 1950s. Peculiarities of local building conditions may lead to the development of a particular style—for instance, the different rowhouse layouts that developed in Boston, New York, Philadelphia, and Washington were based on the cost of plots and the size of the lots laid out as the cities grew in the nineteenth century.

A specific structural or mechanical system becomes a standard because it is an economically rational choice. Any system, no matter how bizarre, may be used in a handful of buildings for reasons that have nothing to do with logic and cost: a designer's insistence on demonstrating a theory, or an owner's insistence on a specific material. For a system to be widely used, it must be the best choice under a frequently occurring set of circumstances. "Best" may mean the least expensive, fastest to build, or the most well suited to a specific use or architectural program. Common circumstances will often lead to the same solutions. Not only do ideas spread through the architectural and engineering press, but also the number of solutions is finite, as most will not work in all situations.

The economic issues are relative. During the twentieth century, building officials in large American cities required that buildings be designed by an architect or engineer regardless of the building type or owner. This requirement goes hand-in-hand with legislated minimum standards of construction, making the client-built building impossible. Many possible solutions to given design problems have therefore been ruled out before the main part of the design process starts. The solutions eliminated tend to be shortcuts: ideas that are inexpensive and expedient but not necessarily safe. Solutions in line with code provisions are usually more complicated than those that are not.

Types can spread from one area to another—usually designers and contractors in a city where construction pressures are high develop a new type as a solution to a specific problem and it spreads first to the neighboring areas and other cities with large amounts of construction, and then across the country (or in some cases the world). Examples of spreading construction technology include steel framing, which moved from Chicago across the Midwest in the 1890s, and cast-iron fronts, which spread from New York in the 1860s. The first is an example of a superior technology gradually driving out its predecessor, while the second is more a case of aggressive businesses (in this case the New York iron foundries) marketing their product.

Building types spread as people in the construction industry look for new markets and tradesmen or design specialists look for better jobs. One advantage for investigators looking to identify building types decades after construction is that types are almost never confined to very small geographical locations, but rather diffuse over large areas.

The Building Envelope

The exterior of a building provides the most obvious architectural image. Even when a building is not deliberately ornamented or is part of a vernacular tradition (for example, the nineteenth-century Cape Cod houses common in small towns), its exterior appearance is a major part of its image. However, in terms of investigation of physical structure, the exterior of a building matters more for its function in keeping out weather. The exterior envelope of a building, comprising the outside walls, the roofs, and roof structures (e.g., dormers) has to keep out water and extremes of temperature.

Exterior walls

There are only a few basic exterior wall types, and their use is clustered in specific building types. The vast majority of wood-stud houses have wood-plank siding (clapboard) or the modern substitutes of aluminum and vinyl siding. Individual boards or their modern-material substitutes slope out and down with their edges lapped to shed water. In masonry houses, as in small masonry buildings in general, the solid masonry walls keep out water. In either case, failure of the wall means failure of the wall materials, and is visible to an inspector through rot or other degradation of siding and cracking and spalling of brick.

Larger buildings may have heavy masonry walls or more modern curtain walls of glass, metal panels, or factory-manufactured masonry panels. Unlike older masonry walls, which keep out water and outside air through the native resistance of the brick, stone, and mortar, modern walls are complex systems that rely on sealants and the interconnection of multiple pieces of wall material at joints. Failure of masonry curtain walls on large buildings, as described in chapter 2, is more complex than the simple failure of the masonry units and mortar; failure of metal and glass curtain walls is even more complex and may not involve actual failure of any single element making up the wall but rather is the failure of the cooperation of components.

Roofing

Keeping water out of a sloped roof is a relatively simple matter, because the water flows with the slope. Seams and gaps in the roofing material can exist in the reverse direction of the water flow without any serious likelihood of leaking. A good example is the use of terra-cotta tile (often called "Spanish tile"): the tiles overlap both in the direction of the water flow, with the bottom of each tile covering the top of the tile below it, and perpendicular to the flow, through the tile shape of interlocked half-circles. Despite the fact that there are gaps in the tile skin, water is deflected down by the tiles and eventually runs off the eave into a gutter or drips to the ground. This ancient technology is still used in construction. More advanced methods of providing a roof exist, but if the color and texture of a tile roof fit the building's architectural scheme, it need not be excluded on technical grounds.

Seamed metal roofing and shingles, made of wood or a substitute such as slate or asphalt, also protect sloped roofs. (Figure 3-1) Like tile roofs, shingles and metal roofing predate the industrial revolution and are still in use because they work.

Flat roofs are far more difficult to waterproof properly than sloped roofs. Even though most "flat" roofs have a slight pitch to force water toward a gutter or drain, water tends to collect and to flow in more than one direction, making a continuous and impermeable waterproofing membrane a necessity.

Most flat roofs use either asphalt-impregnated paper or rubber sheet as the membrane. (Figure 3-2) Since roofing consists of a number of linked elements, there are many variations in construction. Ballast is an

3-1. A traditional slate roof. It was still waterproof when this picture was taken, but the damage to the slates suggests it would be leaking soon. The copper flashing and the gutter support brackets at the eave are intact, but the gutter itself is missing.

3-2. A traditional tar-paper roof in the last stages of failure. The numerous tears in the paper membrane have allowed dirt and water to accumulate, creating a growth medium for moss.

element that provides enough weight to keep the sheets of membrane from lifting up from wind pressure—leading to the familiar "tar and gravel" roof. Insulation is often built into the roof, either below or above the membrane, and secondary membranes may be provided as protection to the actual waterproofing element (cap sheets) or to facilitate attachment of the membrane to the roof structure (base sheets).

The connections of the roofing to the walls are also part of the roof waterproofing. "Flashing" includes a number of different detail elements designed to prevent water from entering the joints between the roofs and the walls and the joints within individual roofs. A typical detail has a piece of metal or cloth (base flashing) that sits under the edge of a roof membrane and curves up at a masonry parapet; a second piece of metal or cloth (cap flashing) is set into the parapet and turns down to cover the edge of the base flashing. Similar details are used at the valleys in roof intersections, at the top of cornices, and around chimneys.

Unless roofing membranes are damaged by improper use (for example, using flat roofs as decks without protection for the waterproofing), the flashing is where an investigation of leaks should begin. As the building moves under load and thermal changes the flashings are subjected to repeated cycles of stress—often the beginning of leaks.

Identifiable Structural Features

The first goal of every investigation is identifying the type of structure within the building. Without knowledge of the structural forms, materials, and details, it is not possible to design or plan renovations and additions. At the most basic level, determining whether the building has a steel frame or joist and bearing wall enables space and use planning, defines possible forms of architectural alteration, and suggests methods of structural alteration. There are several major structural forms and a large number of hybrids, making the careful observation of details and damage the most efficient way to distinguish the types described below.

Note that the descriptions below are classified first by the main vertical load-carrying elements, and second by the floor construction. Other orders are possible and may be just as useful, depending on the location of the building and experience of the investigators. In addition, systems within a single building may be mixed because of different uses within the building, construction phased over time, or sometimes for no discernible reason.

The standard types described here are:

- masonry bearing walls
- wood- and steel-joist floors
- masonry vault floors
- heavy-timber frames
- wood stud
- steel stud
- steel frame
- concrete frame

Other systems may be found, especially in buildings from the nineteenth century, but this list covers the majority of buildings in existence in the United States as of the last half of the twentieth century.

Masonry-bearing-wall buildings

WALLS. In the United States, masonry bearing walls are the oldest form of permanent building, used in many areas for monumental buildings, while wood was used for all typical construction. Because of the simplicity of construction (rough masonry work may require a lot of labor, but not necessarily much skilled labor) and the well-understood performance for buildings of an ordinary size, masonry bearing walls remained the dominant form for urban buildings until the end of the nineteenth century. (Figure 3-3)

3-3. Removal of the plaster on the inside face of a wall has exposed typical nineteenth-century mixed structure. The brick wall is supported over the window by a two-course jack arch; the jack arch was supported during construction by a permanent wood lintel. The wood is now covered with decay fungi.

Most bearing walls are solid masonry, often with a decorative (and relatively expensive) veneer over a plain and inexpensive core. In older buildings, these walls may be roman brick, pressed brick, terra cotta, or stone backed by common brick; in newer buildings, brick, thin stone veneer, stucco, or precast concrete backed by concrete block. In buildings built before 1870, particularly in monumental buildings, thick bearing walls may be built of two layers of veneer with a cheap (often rubble masonry) core.

Cavity walls, where the exterior veneer is separated from the backup by a small air gap, are usually associated with use in skeleton frame buildings, where they are used as nonbearing curtain walls, but have been used occasionally in bearing walls since the 1920s. Cavity walls were first introduced as such around 1900, but they did not gain popularity until after World War II. The delay in their use was based on the meaning of the gap: cavity walls were originally meant to be a way to conserve masonry and provide thermal insulation, but these reasons gradually gave way to the use of the cavity as an element in facade waterproofing. Water that penetrates the outer skin is meant to run down the back face of the veneer or the front face of the backup. Without modern waterproofing materials, it is difficult to properly waterproof the backup and to provide flashing to channel the water where necessary.

Cavity walls require much more careful detailing to direct the water that penetrates the veneer. Improper details, especially when located at the tops and sides of windows, may result in water damage to the windows, backup masonry, or interior finishes. The gap is often used as a location for the building's insulation, creating the possibility of differential thermal movement between the veneer and backup.

Before the 1910s, when modern-style reinforced concrete became standardized across the United States, foundations were usually some form of masonry. Early concrete foundations are sometimes unreinforced and resemble, in both design and form, masonry foundations. Masonry foundation types include rough-cut granite, limestone, or schist rubble, coursed rubble (where the rubble is partially squared off to allow more regular arrangement), brick, concrete block, and cast-in-place concrete. (Figure 3-4)

The main items of concern in masonry-wall construction are water damage and the method of original design used. All masonry is subject to mortar deterioration through the loss of cement and masonry body dete-

3-4. The original construction includes the mid-nineteenth-century rubble foundation wall; the piping is easily identified as later additions by its awkward location cutting into the door's arched head and passing through the wall.

rioration caused by cracking and spalling. Both cement loss and body deterioration are caused by exposure to water, particularly the freeze-thaw cycles in temperate or cold climates. Rubble foundations are particularly vulnerable to joint washout when constantly exposed to water: their relatively wide joints facilitate water penetration, and their irregular shapes are physically unstable when the mortar is damaged. Brick foundations are somewhat more rare, but they are more porous and more subject to material degradation. Brick foundations are more stable than rubble until they are badly damaged by water, at which time they gradually turn back to the clay from which the brick was first made.

In general, masonry walls were not actually designed for their applied loads until the twentieth century. Even after engineering design had been applied to building elements, masonry walls often continued to be sized using rules of thumb and code-mandated thicknesses. The rules governing the required thicknesses of masonry walls in late-nineteenth-century building codes are long and complex, reflecting the conflicting needs to make the rules usable for builders with no engineering training and to have a rational design that reflected the actual stresses within the walls. In cases where the loads are being changed by an alteration, particularly when the introduction of new framing will place concentrated loads on the walls, the strength of masonry to resist the loads must be reviewed in detail.

FLOORS. As masonry bearing walls are the oldest, most traditional form of vertical support and exterior enclosure for large and permanent buildings, the most common associated floor structures are wood-joist floors. These floors are similar to solid masonry bearing walls: they are simple and repetitive forms, require little skilled labor during construction, and are designed based on rules of thumb and tradition. Masonry vault floors, despite their superficial similarity to masonry walls, are far more difficult to build and require specialized knowledge of arches. Vaults have typically been used only in monumental buildings and in areas where wood is inappropriate because of exposure.

Joists are small beams, nominally 2 or 3 inches wide and 8 to 14 inches deep. The most common spacing is 16 inches on center, although spacings of 12 inches on center for heavily loaded or long-span floors and 24 inches on center for unoccupied roofs are both common.

Wood joists are usually supported on masonry walls by having their ends embedded into separate pockets within the masonry, although in older buildings they may be supported by a wood beam (a "ledger") bolted parallel to the masonry face, and in the twentieth century, by steel shelf angles bolted to the masonry. In most cases, wood joists support a wood plank (or after the 1940s, plywood) subfloor. At kitchens and bathrooms, where the floor is expected to be wet occasionally and where tile floors are common, the wood joists may support a wood subfloor set below the top of the joists that serves as a platform to hold concrete or mortar fill. This fill ("deafening") and the associated complexity of building the dropped subfloor ("deafened joists") has fallen out of favor since 1950. The modern solution is to use shallower joists supporting a continuous plywood subfloor to which tiles are glued or, in better construction, set in mortar.

Certain details specific to the type are required for the use of wood-joist floors. Wherever openings through the floor are required for stairs, elevators, ducts, or other vertical nonstructural building elements, the joists must be cut short. A beam called a header runs perpendicular to the joists at the edge of the opening to carry the short joists; the header is carried at each end by an enlarged joist called a trimmer. Headers and trimmers, by tradition, are made of two joists running side by side. Double-joist headers and trimmers are ordinarily adequate for openings up to 6 or 8 feet in length, but structural analysis of existing conditions often shows that the headers are overstressed.

Wood-to-wood connections are required where the joists meet the header, where the header meets the trimmer, and sometimes elsewhere. Before 1900, most of these connections were made with mortise and tenon, where the end of the supported member was cut down to a small tongue that was inserted into a hole cut in the supporting member. (Figure 3-5) While it yields an acceptable connection that can withstand low stress, cutting the end of the supported member into the tenon produces shear stress concentration that can lead to horizontal cracking, while the mortise hole in the supporting member creates bending stress concentrations that can lead to horizontal and vertical cracking. The next stage in connection was the development of the "bridle iron" in the late-nineteenth century. (Figure 3-6) This is an iron or steel strap bent so that it hooks over the supporting member and cradles the supported member. Bridles eliminated the need to cut the wood, although they did tend to introduce torsion into the supporting member. When overloaded, bridles twist the supporting member, possibly to the point of failure. Bridles were gradually (although not entirely) phased out in favor of similarly designed connectors made of sheet steel, usually called "joist hangers."

When wood joists are supported in pockets in a masonry wall, the ends are shaped with a "fire-cut." This detail entails cutting the end of the joist so that it slopes back roughly 15 degrees from vertical, which prevents the top surface of the joist from extending into the wall. Fire-cuts were developed in the late nineteenth century to prevent a specific type of collapse: when the joists of a joist floor burn through during a fire, they no longer span across the building, and will start to fall down in the center. If the joist ends are solidly embedded in the wall, they will push the wall upward as they rotate down, which cracks the wall and pulls it down into the building. Fire-cut joists are free to rotate and will collapse without damaging the wall. While this obviously matters only in the middle of a serious fire, it can greatly reduce the amount of damage to the building and,

3-5. Removal of the plank floor shows, at left, a mortise-and-tenon connection typical of the original 1840s construction and, at center, expanded metal lath supporting the plaster ceiling of the space below from a 1930s alteration.

3-6. At the bottom center a bridle iron supports a double header (to allow passage of the chimney at the right through the floor) from a double trimmer.

more important, reduce the number of fatalities among anyone still in the building, including firemen.

Traditional floor construction for monumental buildings was solid masonry vaulting, matching the bearing walls in weight and thickness, if not strength. Because masonry is incapable of withstanding tension, and therefore incapable of spanning large horizontal distances in the manner of a beam, arched vaults are the most common type of masonry floor. Even though most floors of this type were built to rules of thumb and not actually designed, they tend to be extremely strong and stable as long as the horizontal thrust produced at the end of the vaults is adequately restrained by walls. Damage to this type of construction is usually associated with large-scale foundation movement, failure of the walls, or extreme weathering. Unlike modern steel and concrete structures, which can be seriously damaged by small foundation movements, a well-built masonry building can withstand small movements through the redistribution of loads caused when the masonry settles into a new position. The same lack of solid connection between individual pieces of masonry that makes resisting tension impossible allows small movements to occur without damage.

Other floor systems are found in bearing-wall buildings, including the use of light-gage steel joists in a manner similar to wood joists, the use of "open-web" steel joists, steel beams functioning as major supporting elements, and the use of cast-in-place and precast concrete slabs.

Light-gage joist floors are most commonly found in small commercial and light industrial buildings that are often one story high. Because of the expansion of the light-gage steel industry and price fluctuations in cut lumber, this type of construction is often seen in houses built after 1985.

Open-web steel joists (also called bar joists) are small trusses placed at a regular spacing of 2 to 4 feet. The members that make up the trusses are small angles (usually with legs no longer than 2 inches) and round steel bars. The joists are premanufactured to length, so they can be simply set in place on site in the same manner as light-gage joists. Because of the difficulty in making connections between two open-web joists, they are usually used with steel beams as headers and trimmers. Open-web joists can bear in small pockets in a masonry wall or on the top flange of a steel beam, so no special connections are required for their use.

The combination of steel (or wrought-iron) beams and masonry bearing walls goes back to the 1840s, but certain problems inherent in the construction have never been entirely solved. For the beams to be seated properly, they should extend at least 8 inches into the wall (in order to engage at least two wythes of brick), but in order for the beams to be reasonably well protected against weathering, they should be at least 4 inches, and preferably more, from the outside face of the wall. These conditions are not mutually exclusive, but unless the walls are (by modern standards) very thick, the conditions can be difficult to satisfy simultaneously, leading to beam ends too close to the outside face or localized masonry crushing on the inside face below the base plate.

Steel beams, by themselves, do not supply a floor. When used in a bearing-wall building, the beams span between walls and support the actual floor. Possible secondary floor elements are the same as those for steel-frame buildings: wood joist, light-gage joist, masonry floors, and concrete slabs. None of these systems is particularly common because there is little logic in introducing large amounts of steel work into a bearing-wall building: steel is used for its strength and rapid erection, while masonry is used for its simplicity and low cost. It is not possible to combine the good qualities of the two systems: a building that requires the time of bearing masonry to complete, has low lateral strength, and costs nearly as much as a steel frame has few attractions. The presence of a small number of steel beams—for example, to continue the line of bearing for joists over a door opening in a masonry wall—is much more easily justified.

Buildings with steel beams supported on bearing walls and supporting wood or light-gage joists are usually one-story commercial buildings. If the building is wide enough, there will be interior steel columns or masonry piers. If there are perimeter columns, they are often tied into the facades through built-in masonry piers; the alternate is masonry piers built into the perimeter walls, in line with the interior columns or piers. While this is a serviceable building, it tends to have the worst characteristics of all of the materials used in terms of weathering and lateral load resistance.

A construction system consisting of masonry bearing walls, steel beam (or wrought-iron beam) and concrete-slab floors has been used to some degree, particularly in the late nineteenth and early twentieth centuries, when steel construction was relatively more expensive than it is now. All types of buildings were built this way, including apartment houses and office towers, but the system lasted the longest with heavy industrial buildings. A variation on this system is the use of masonry floors, mostly commonly brick arch, and terra-cotta tile. Brick arch was most common in factories with high floor loads and impact. The use of tile arch is described at greater length in the section on steel-frame buildings.

The combination of masonry bearing walls and concrete-beam-and-slab floors is quite rare. In the era when bearing walls were most popular for their simplicity, before 1920, concrete was still considered a high-tech solution. In more modern construction, bearing walls are used on small buildings, where cast-in-place concrete is usually avoided to keep costs down. But in the 1890s and 1900s—a transition period for both masonry-bearing-wall construction and reinforced concrete design—this combination may have been used to create floors with a high load capacity and that were relatively impervious to weathering. Because of the infrequent use of the combination, and its use when concrete was in its infancy, the details of construction were not always very well thought out. For example, there may be little or no physical tie between the concrete and the masonry.

The system of concrete-block bearing walls and precast-concrete "plank" floors was developed in the last half of the twentieth century and used heavily in certain fields where cost and durability were the primary consideration. The system was used for a great deal of low-rise, low-cost housing and low-rise commercial and industrial space where large, open spaces were not required. The advantage to it is that it requires little off-site fabrication: the masonry walls are built up block by block (or brick by brick), the concrete plank is laid on top, and concrete poured at the joints to tie the pieces together. Reinforcement is placed in the concrete and extends into the plank and into the block above and below in order to provide continuity in the joints. This reinforcement is the critical element in providing lateral stability, and its improper construction can cause problems ranging from collapse to cracking finishes both on the interior and exterior. Block and plank buildings require much more reinforcement when designed for seismic conditions because of the difficulty in creating continuity; as seismic requirements have spread across the United States from the high seismic zones on the West Coast, this style has gradually fallen out of favor. In particular, the earthquake in Armenia in 1988 damaged the reputation of this system, as thousands of people died in poorly built apartment houses of this type.

Wood-frame buildings

Heavy wood frames are the oldest form of wood construction in buildings and bear a distant relationship to modern steel-frame buildings. Wood-frame buildings have large wood posts carrying wood beams and girders and, most importantly, some form of bracing connecting the various elements. The braces provide lateral stability to the frame, allowing the exterior walls to be simple, nonload-bearing enclosures. The braces may be heavy timbers (nearly as large as the main posts) running at an angle between posts and beams, they may be smaller, repetitive members (some heavy timber frames use wood-stud walls as bracing elements), or, in modern buildings, they may be some form of metal strap. Heavy timber framing was relatively rare in the United States after 1850 except in barns and some types of mills, but it was more common in Europe. The appearance of half-timbered construction, where the timbers are set within a stuccoed wall and visible as vertical, horizontal, and diagonal strips, shows the separation of the load-bearing (wood) structure and the nonload-bearing (stucco over brick or lath) enclosure.

While ordinarily an adequate form of structure, the use of heavy wood frames was effectively ended in the United States by the development of "stick" (cut lumber) forms: the balloon frame and its later derivative, the platform frame. (See the section on wood-stud buildings that follows). The continued use of heavy frames for barns was the result of the balloon frame's inability to maintain lateral stability when large holes are cut in the walls for wide doors and when large open spaces are required on the interior. Heavy frames, with their knee braces, were equally stable with solid plank walls, lattice walls, or openings, and so were well-suited for barn and storage building use. In addition, barns do not have to be constructed to the same standards as houses: people will complain if their floors and walls are not level and plumb, while the occupants of barns tend not to care.

Heavy timber frames were used for industrial buildings longer than for other building types in part because of their good fire resistance. Wood is not a material associated with good performance in a fire, but large-section timbers do not burn very quickly. A factory built entirely of heavy timbers (with floors made of very thick planks supported on heavy timbers) is more resistant to fire than one built with masonry walls and thin wood-joist floors.

The most common problem with wood braced frames is failure of the lateral bracing. Since the stability of the frame is dependent on the connections between the braces and the posts and between the braces and the beams, damage to the connections can cause failure of the entire building. The common carpenters' connections—mortise-and-tenon connections and individual metal bolts and wood pins—are generally inadequate when exposed to wood shrinkage, load reversal, and the stress concentrations caused by the connection configurations. Over time, the braces often "loosen," allowing the frame to lean out of plumb. The lean itself puts further strain on the connections, accelerating unrepaired damage.

There are two forms of built-in resistance to damage that buildings of this type have: accidental bracing and extreme exposure to weather. Many of these buildings have survived because the exterior walls or interior partitions accidentally serve as bracing diaphragms supplementing the action of the braces. In addition, the fungi that most commonly destroy wood are less likely to grow when exposed to low temperatures and fresh air. So the exposure of interior structure through the lack of finishes and temperature regulation, qualities that greatly reduce the utility of the buildings for human occupancy, help to reduce weathering damage.

Wood-stud buildings

This form of wood construction is distinguished by four substitutions: small, repetitive wood studs substituted for large posts; small, repetitive wood joists for large beams; small braces or sheathing connected to the studs for large knee braces; and wire nails in direct connection and light-gage steel joist hangers for pins and mortise-and-tenon connections. The use of large numbers of cut-lumber members and of wire nails marked some of the earliest industrialization of the building process. The introduction of inexpensive cut lumber ("sticks") and wire nails in the 1840s allowed the natural advantages of stud framing to make it the most popular type of wood construction. These advantages include the small size and light weight of the individual pieces, the direct connections (eliminating the need for complex cutting of mortise and tenons), and the lower costs associated with lumber that could be cut from small trees.

Freestanding private houses are by far the most common wood-stud-and-joist buildings. They are rarely engineered as individual buildings: joist tables, standard details, and roof-truss computer programs make structural designers unnecessary. (Figure 3-7) While these are spoken of

3-7. Wood framing in a house that has undergone repeated alteration. The newest framing is the wood-stud partition near the camera, which must be load-bearing, since the joists above have been cut and inadequately spliced.

as wood stud, they may contain heavy timber beams, nonstandard roof trusses, engineered lumber, individual steel beams or steel-and-wood flitch plates, or structural masonry walls not obvious from external observation. Many of the most common problems arise from sloppy construction, including a lack of foundation tie-downs ("hurricane anchors"), a lack of rafter tie-downs, and toe nailing of connections instead of gage straps or end nailing.

There are two basic types of wood-stud house: balloon frame and platform frame. The balloon frame, which is characterized by two-story-high studs supporting the second floor on a ledger beam usually called a ribband, was the first type of stick framing developed. The platform frame is characterized by entirely separate framing of each level, so that after the second-floor structure is complete it serves as a work platform from which the second-floor studs and roof can be built. Both types yield well-built houses.

Foundations for new wood-stud houses are typically cast-in-place concrete or concrete block. The outer surface of the concrete or block is covered with waterproofing and possibly insulation. Block is more vulnerable in climates with below-freezing temperatures, as the voids in the block, even if grouted, may collect water, which causes damage during freeze-thaw cycles. The foundations of older houses may be brick or rubble masonry, both of which are difficult to waterproof, but are more inherently waterproof than modern concrete block. Foundations for porches are often small piers of masonry subject to settlement and deterioration from ground water; garages and other areas without basements or crawl spaces usually have a concrete slab on grade floor. Houses in frost-free environments may have only slabs on grade for foundations; the required depth of the foundations is directly related to the amount of frost expected.

The construction of a typical wood-frame house varies depending on whether the house was built singly or as part of a development. Developers' construction of groups of nearly identical houses began in the nineteenth century with urban rowhouses, usually with masonry walls, and was later extended to wood-frame houses both inside and outside cities. The groups may be as small as three or four houses, or as large as hundreds. There have been cases of entire towns being built at once (the Levittowns built after World War II in New Jersey, Pennsylvania, and New York are excellent examples), but in terms of examining single buildings there is no difference between a development of a hundred houses and one of a thousand.

Houses built as part of a large group typically have simplified construction details, regardless of how complex the architectural design is. Even though each house must still be individually built, part of the logic behind building large groups of houses is to take advantage of economies of scale in materials and unskilled labor. Group-built houses are more likely to have prefabricated roof trusses, standardized sizes of lumber for joists and rafters (regardless of the stresses), and steel beams or other specialized framing. It may be difficult to justify the expense of bringing in steel workers for a single beam because the set-up costs would far exceed the actual cost of the beam, but if fifty identical beams are to be installed, the set-up costs can be spread out and become less important.

The types of damage common to houses are better known than those for any other building type because so many people have experienced them firsthand. The most common are various forms of minor foundation failure, including seepage through improper waterproofing, porous masonry in contact with earth drawing water up through capillary action (rising damp), settlement of minor elements such as porch-pier foundations, and cracking due to local overstress near basement windows or other irregularities. Damage to the wood frame itself can include joists and beams being overstressed due to improper design, overstress and splitting poor-quality wood, and deterioration from attack by fungi and insects.

There are a number of possible design flaws more complicated than simple beam overstress. Joists or beams are sometimes designed properly for stress but undersized for deflection, which creates excessive deflection. Because wood has a tendency to "creep"—that is, undergo long-term deflection under constant load—old wood floor joists may pick up a curved shape (visible as "dished" and sloping floors). This is not a sign of overstress or improper design and usually cannot be removed.

Gable roofs have a tendency to spread if they are not tied by attic joists, which push the tops of the walls outward. (Figure 3-8) Dormers, hips, and valleys in the roof may not be properly designed, creating stress concentrations at the beams at the edge. Masonry chimneys sometimes deteriorate or, more seriously, may not be properly flashed to the surrounding

3-8. Poor quality repairs and alterations at the eave connection of rafters and attic joists to the exterior stud wall. Note also the lack of a true header beam over the window at left—the only support for the eave above is a pair of 2x4s turned on the flat.

roof, allowing water into the wood framing. Any stress or deterioration problem will be visible as split wood, excessive deflections, and staining.

A subtle design flaw is the improper use of insulation and vapor barriers. Modern wood-frame houses tend to be much "tighter" than ones built before the 1970s energy crisis. This includes the use of double-glazed insulating windows, heavy insulation within the exterior stud walls, and more complete ventilation equipment that reduces the dependence on outside air. Separate from the debate over whether or not sealed houses are bad for the occupants is the effect of this type of construction on the building. When the temperatures on the inside and outside of a building are very different (either much colder on the outside during the winter or much colder on the inside during the summer), it is possible that the dew point, the temperature at which water vapor in the warmer air begins to condense, will be reached within the exterior walls. Condensation within the walls is a great threat to the longevity of the wood studs, so a plastic "vapor barrier" is provided within the wall to collect the water and carry it down to the bottom of the wall and out of the building. Rot in the exterior walls, including stains on the inside and local failures of exterior sheathing from rot around nails, signifies potential problems with the vapor barrier. This problem is most serious in areas with temperate climates: no single vapor-barrier location is going to be correct for hot, humid summers and cold winters, making some condensation a recurring problem for many houses.

Finally, the great flaw in wood houses is their lack of fire resistance. A common belief among design professionals and firefighters is that if a wood house has not yet had a fire, it will eventually. Damage can vary from negligible to the complete loss of the building, but small fires often cause local damage that is then improperly repaired. When a small area of floor joists or wall studs is found to be oriented incorrectly or is wildly different from the adjacent framing, it is quite probable that the area in question is a fire repair.

Steel-stud buildings

Light-gage steel studs and joists (often called C-joists) are used as substitutes for wood studs and joists. Most steel-stud buildings greatly resemble wood-stud buildings in configuration and load capacity. The details of steel-stud construction differ from wood stud largely in two ways. First, because the studs and joists are made of light-gage steel that is less than

⅛ inch thick, stiffeners must be provided at connections to prevent deformation of the C-shaped stud and joist sections. Second, direct connection of members can be achieved by screwing through the web or flange of one member into another.

Concrete slabs over light-gage metal deck can be easily installed over steel-joist floors, creating a building type not possible in wood. This provides a sturdier floor and creates a better fire separation between floors than the typical plywood subfloor, but it does not automatically create a fire-rated building because protecting the light-gage studs from the heat of fire is difficult.

One-story commercial buildings can be constructed using steel studs and joists and plain, light-gage steel deck as the roof. Because this material does not provide even the stiffness or sound insulation of plywood, it is not suitable for interior floors. The steel deck may be covered by insulation below the waterproofing.

As noted above with bearing-wall construction, light-gage steel has, roughly since 1985, been used for private houses. This is most common at times when the cost of lumber is high; the unit cost of a steel joist is almost always higher than the cost of a similar size and strength wood joist, but the cost of creating connections in steel is usually lower.

The design of steel-stud buildings is similar to the design of wood-stud buildings in that it rarely involves much engineering. Joist sizes are picked from load tables and connection details from manufacturers' recommendations for typical connections, including lateral bracing from exterior wall sheathing or strap braces attached to the studs.

Long-term weathering poses the most serious threat to light-gage construction. Rusting of steel takes place at the exposed surface, so a thin piece of steel with a high surface-to-volume ratio loses strength from rusting much faster than a thick piece of steel. Unprotected light-gage studs and joists rapidly become useless when exposed to water or damp air, which is the reason that most structural light-gage members are galvanized. The galvanized protection makes light-gage a viable construction material, but any source of water is potentially a serious problem.

Steel-frame buildings
Steel skeleton frames can be found in most of the most prominent high-rise buildings in the United States as well as in many smaller buildings, including one-story, nondescript commercial and industrial structures.

Between 1910 and 1950, nearly every mid- and high-rise building in the United States was built with a steel frame; while the complete dominance of steel has ended, it is still commonly used for multistoried buildings. The defining characteristic of the type—the use of structural steel for columns, lateral bracing, and floor beams—first appeared in the United States in the 1880s and reached a mature form by the 1910s.

Three identification issues beyond the simple presence of a steel frame should be addressed: the type of lateral bracing, the type of floor structure, and the type of exterior wall. The second and third are vital pieces of information, while the first is useful in identifying the causes of damage but may be difficult to determine.

Steel frames are broken into two categories by the type of lateral bracing: braced frames and unbraced, or moment, frames. Braced frames include diagonal braces that run from one floor to the next at every floor. Unbraced frames are braced by rigid connections between beams and columns. Braced-frame buildings have less sidesway under lateral load than unbraced-frame buildings of a similar size. Excess sidesway may be noticeable to tenants and can damage nonstructural building elements. The type of bracing is often hard to determine: diagonal braces are usually hidden in partitions surrounding elevators or other portions of the core, while the rigid connections for unbraced frames are hidden within the floor structure. The easiest way to find information on bracing without performing probes is to look in mechanical spaces, especially those at lower or mid-height floors. Because mechanical rooms are open and have few partitions, diagonal bracing may be visible.

A steel frame alone is not a usable building because it has no floors or walls. This may seem obvious, but it is in direct contrast to the masonry-bearing-wall, wood-joist-floor structure that steel has replaced. Once the masonry and wood have been assembled, this older type of structure has floors and walls that create a usable, if barren, shell. Three types of floor have been used with steel frames: joist, masonry, and concrete. Concrete is historically the most common and is used for the floors of nearly all modern steel buildings.

Wood and light-gage joist floors never have been popular in combination with steel frames. If the owners, designers, and contractors go to the trouble and expense of designing and erecting a steel frame, the goals for the project usually include a fire-rated assembly and "solid-feeling" floors. Because wood-joist floors are flammable, they are excluded from most fired-rated construction. Light-gage steel joists, though they are nonflammable, are still excluded from most rated floor systems. Therefore, open-web joists supporting a thin concrete slab make up the majority of joist floors used with steel-frame buildings. Joist floors have several undesirable properties, all stemming from the fact that they are much lighter than concrete slab floors. Joist floors tend to move more than other floors under load, even loads as small as a single person walking, making them feel "bouncy." Since most of the space in a joist floor is empty, noise and odors will transmit through if there are any small gaps in the ceiling and subfloor. Unlike the strong and fairly rigid connections that can be made between two members of structural steel, wood and light-gage joist connections to steel beams are very flexible. The usual method of connection is with joist hangers, although the practice of fitting the end of the joist between the beam flanges still exists even though it creates a weak and potentially unstable connection. Finally, joist floors cannot provide much rigidity in the plane of the floor to the steel beams, so secondary, horizontal bracing may be needed. Most steel buildings with joist floors are one-story commercial buildings, in which the joists are used to create the roof. In these buildings, the weaknesses of joist construction rarely are a problem.

Masonry floors were used in the earliest wrought-iron and steel-frame buildings. When metal framing was first developed, in the late nineteenth century, concrete construction had not yet progressed to the point where its use for floors in large buildings was feasible, and no other method of constructing floors existed. The last and most popular type of masonry floor, the terra-cotta tile arch, was in regular use until roughly 1920. Masonry floors required the use of wood formwork and individual placement of each masonry unit, making this type of construction labor intensive and expensive. Because all of these floors are arches of some type, they must be fairly thick and solid, making them wasteful of space and difficult to use in combination with modern utilities.

The oldest type of infill floor for metal-frame construction is the brick arch. These floors were less efficient in terms of material, labor, and space than tile arches, so the development of tile in the 1870s drove out brick arches except in areas of high exposure to water, such as sidewalk vaults. (Figure 3-9) In those areas, the brick usually survives better than the beams supporting it: water degrades the mortar and the brick bodies, but because the brick is porous, the water runs out through the bottom. In

3-9. The brick-arch floor support on iron beams above this 1870s basement also supports more recent additions, such as the sprinkler system and fluorescent lights.

floors, however, the brick works like a sponge and holds the water against the beams. Structural overload is nearly impossible, as the beams will fail from bending overstress long before the arches fail from compression overstress.

The replacement for the brick arch was the tile arch. There are many types, all of which are basically arches spanning between iron or steel beams. The beams are tied together horizontally with rods to prevent movement from the arch thrust. Covered by fill and often wood flooring on sleepers, the arch tops show few signs of damage. Most of the floors are "flat arches" with horizontal top and bottom surfaces. The bottoms are either covered with plaster or protected by a hung ceiling. In plastered floors, movement from lack of thrust bracing or overload may be visible, but it is not likely. The less common segmental arches have a cross-section that is a circular arc; therefore, they have deeper fill over the beams (the spring points of the arch) and must have hung ceilings to create a flat bottom. The most common form of damage to tile arches is degradation of the bottom surface of the tile from the insertion of hangers for plumbing, ducts, and ceilings.

Concrete slabs replaced tile arches in the first two decades of the twentieth century, although early concrete slabs may be very different from those of modern construction. Ultimately, concrete slabs have proved to be the best combination with steel frames, as they contribute a stable fire-resistant floor. (Figure 3-10)

Before the 1950s, most concrete slabs were solid concrete, placed over temporary formwork. In general, solid concrete floor slabs (often referred to as "formed concrete" to distinguish them from slabs on metal deck, which don't require formwork) are as strong or stronger than slabs on metal deck and also are as weather resistant. The exception to this is a type of slab popular from 1910 to 1940: the cinder-concrete, draped-mesh slab. This type of floor, which was extremely popular in its time and can be found in thousands of buildings, uses wire mesh instead of rebar for its reinforcing and uses concrete made with coal cinder instead of gravel as coarse aggregate. These slabs are as strong or stronger than bar-reinforced stone concrete slabs, but they are extremely vulnerable to water for three reasons: the concrete tends to be porous, allowing water on top

3-10. Most of the steel in this 1930 office building is encased in concrete, as it was originally built. In some areas, modern spray-on fireproofing (appearing as gray "oatmeal") covers the steel, strongly suggesting recent alterations.

of the slab to penetrate everywhere; the coal cinders may contain sulfur, which actively attacks the steel mesh when wet; and the wire mesh, with a high surface-area-to-volume ratio, is more vulnerable to corrosion than larger steel bar would be. Cinder-concrete floor slabs (recognizable by the black and brittle cinders in their bottom surfaces) always must be carefully inspected for signs of water damage. (Figure 3-11)

The most common floor system for modern steel-frame construction is that of concrete slabs over corrugated steel deck. The deck is a light-gage material, easy to transport and cut to shape in the field, and usually serves as both the form for the wet concrete and as reinforcing, bound to the concrete through the design of the corrugation ridges. Various combinations of concrete weight, deck gage, and deck thicknesses are used. The system is recognizable from below through the shape of the deck, even when coated with spray-on fireproofing. The structural system itself is resilient, although if it is improperly designed, excessive deflections or vibrations can cause cracking in attached ceilings, floor finishes, and partitions. The metal deck, whether galvanized or not, will rust rapidly after

3-11. Failure of a concrete slab reinforced with draped mesh. The concrete below the mesh plane has spalled as the mesh has rusted. The first sign of a problem was cracking and peeling of the plaster below the concrete.

long-term exposure to water. Deck is usually protected by a coating (galvanizing, paint, or fireproofing) and should not be directly exposed to weathering.

Wire-mesh reinforcing is usually installed in concrete on metal deck floors to control shrinkage cracking in the top surface of the slab. This mesh is supposed to be near the top surface of the slab but is often too low, either from being misplaced or because it moved down under the weight of wet concrete dumped on it during construction. Improperly located mesh results in a network of fine cracks in the slab top. The cracks are a nuisance but do not represent a structural failure or change in strength.

A fast and relatively inexpensive floor system for steel-frame construction is precast concrete plank. The planks are 6- to 12-inch-thick slabs, usually with hollow cores, reinforced and cast in factories, and lifted into place on site by a crane. Left bare, they create ugly and uneven floors, so they are usually covered with cast-in-place concrete fill. However, if both fill and a hung ceiling are used, the additional work required removes much of the economic advantage of plank over slabs on metal deck. The planks come from the factory with embedded metal clips for attachment to the steel beams. If the clips are improperly cast in, there may be severe cracking at the attachments. The underside of this floor system is often left bare or covered with "popcorn" paint; the visible joints between the slabs clearly indicate the floor type.

Concrete-joist and waffle-slab floors, as described in detail in the following section on concrete-frame buildings, are rare in steel-frame buildings because they tend to be deeper than the steel beams and because of the logistical difficulties in using complex concrete floors in steel frames. One type of concrete-joist floor used in steel frames with some regularity from the 1890s to the 1940s was the tile-infilled joist. There were many variations, but the essential idea was a sequence of construction and material use: after the steel was erected, wood forms were built below the beams. Terra-cotta tiles, concrete blocks, or some other form of hollow masonry unit were placed on the forms in parallel strips, defining the joists as voids. Rebar was placed between the blocks, and concrete was placed as filling between the blocks and sometimes over them as well. In all of these systems, the blocks remained in place permanently. After the concrete cured, the forms were removed, creating a concrete-joist floor with masonry permanently filling the inter-joist voids. Once metal deck became available in the 1950s, these types of joist floors fell out of favor because of the extra expense required in building the forms.

One of the defining characteristics of a modern steel-frame building is that the exterior walls are supported by the frame. The floor beams at the outside edges of the building (spandrel beams) are both part of the interior floor system and part of the exterior wall support. Exterior walls that are supported and therefore do not carry load for more than one floor are all technically "curtain walls," but that term is often used only for walls made primarily of glass and light metal systems. Curtain walls can be masonry and appear as heavy as bearing walls.

In steel-frame construction, the curtain wall type (including its attachment method) most greatly influences weathering damage and the visibility of movement damage. A poorly designed curtain wall will leak, move improperly (or fail to move when it should—when the building frame moves under load), and will deteriorate rapidly from weathering. Poor details can trap water, allow glass or metal panels to come loose, and permit drafts of outside air. Complaints from building occupants about drafts, leaks, and peculiar noises near the exterior walls should be taken as evidence that the curtain walls may be failing or inadequate, regardless of the overall condition of the building.

Concrete-frame buildings

Unlike steel-frame buildings, which developed gradually from wrought-iron frames (and even further from timber frames), reinforced concrete in the United States was a modern system from its first use. Most of the early development of the material and its use as a system for whole-building frames took place in Europe. From the viewpoint of an American in 1910, the use of reinforced concrete to create entire building frames appeared full-grown and unified. Some of the early beam designs resembled those in other materials, but detailing and design theory were inherently different from the start.

The most obvious use of concrete is for floor slabs, first in steel-frame buildings and then as part of entire reinforced concrete frames. Floors in steel-frame buildings and in many concrete-frame buildings from before 1940 consist of one-way slabs—slabs that act like beams, carrying load to two supports at opposing ends. When one-way slabs are used in concrete-frame buildings, they typically span between beams, which may be supported by columns, walls, or girders. This type of system, which resembles

3-12. The bottom of this floor slab from a 1930 building shows the marks of board forms. Visual observation does not ordinarily reveal reinforcing type, but in this case the small hole (stuffed with a paper bag) clearly shows the wire mesh reinforcing.

the layout of a steel-frame building, does not take full advantage of the unique properties of concrete (continuity and lack of geometric constraints) and is less efficient in construction than other types of concrete floor requiring less formwork. Concrete is unique among structural materials in that it is cast in place, with no inherent shape of its own. This is an advantage in creating complex shapes and reducing the amount of shop fabrication, but it makes the construction of temporary formwork on site into a significant portion of the construction process. Before 1950, most formwork was built of wood plank (plywood has been used since then), although reusable steel forms have been used for some construction roughly since 1900. (Figure 3-12) Concrete will pick up irregularities in the surface of the forms—the underside of a slab will show the edges of planks in the form of low ridges, and knots in plywood will be clearly visible in relief. This property provides rough information about a slab's age.

Combinations of one-way slabs and beams require complex formwork that takes longer to build and may be as expensive as the concrete itself. This economic disadvantage has greatly reduced the system's popularity, particularly since 1950. However, buildings with one of the more efficient floor systems described may have small areas of beam and one-way slab construction, particularly in irregularly shaped bays or near floor openings for elevators, stairs, or mechanical equipment. For this reason, identification of the floor types should take place in the middle of a typical floor area, where the basic type will be visible.

All reinforced concrete construction depends on transferring stress to the rebar through concrete cracking. Changes in theory during the course of the twentieth century have resulted in steadily greater requirements for reinforcing at certain locations, especially at the top of beams and slabs at supports. Older buildings may show heavy cracking in slab tops near beams. These cracks are visible proof of stress distribution, not failure, but if they grow too large they can reduce the water and fire protection that the concrete provides for the rebar.

Most concrete slabs cannot span long distances because they are not deep enough. Stress and deflection increase far more rapidly than the span length does, so a 4- to 6-inch one-way slab is usually only adequate for spans in the range of 10 to 15 feet. The use of cast-in-place concrete-joist floors allows for long spans with simple formwork. The joists are small, narrow beams, usually less than 2 feet deep, spaced less than 3 feet on center, cast integrally with a thin slab. Early joist designs used blocks made of terra cotta, cinders, and concrete block permanently cast into the slab. The blocks reduced the amount of concrete required. By the 1930s the use of reusable steel forms to create the voids between joists had become the standard. Unlike the complex formwork required for one-way slabs and ordinary beams, forms for joist floors are simple, flat planes, with the reusable void forms placed on top.

"Two-way" slabs or "flat slab" floors are unique to reinforced concrete construction. Because concrete can be cast in any shape for which formwork can be constructed, and will carry load in any direction for which reinforcing is required, more complex designs than simple one-way beams and slabs can be designed and built. Two-way slabs are rectangular sections of floor, usually nearly square in proportion, that span between supports located on all four sides. The structural design methods for this type of floor are fairly complicated, as they have to take into account bending in both directions.

Flat-slab design relies heavily on continuity and stress distribution through deflection. As a result, cracks in both the top and bottom surfaces of the slabs may appear in unexpected locations, especially when the slabs have irregular shapes. This is an ordinary part of concrete construction and not, in itself, a cause for alarm. Small investigations are often triggered by the presence of these cracks.

The term "flat slab" is something of a misnomer, since nearly all concrete floor slabs are flat. The term refers to the relative absence of beams projecting from the bottom of the floor. There may be beams running from one column to another, defining the edge of each floor panel, as well as two forms of reinforcing near the columns: drop panels and column capitals. Drop panels, usually square in plan, are thicker areas of slab located around each column. They provide additional strength in bending to resist the high moments and shears near the slab supports. Column capitals, usually truncated cones in shape, are the structural concrete version of the ornamental capitals on classical stone columns. Capitals provide additional shear resistance near the columns. In heavily loaded floors, capitals may be used in conjunction with drop panels.

Many patented and peculiarly reinforced types of flat slab were used from 1900 to 1930: for example, the "three-way" system, which provided reinforcing spanning in two directions at right angles and reinforcing spanning diagonally across slab panels from one column to another. Flat slabs with beams, drop panels, and capitals have fallen out of use since the introduction of plywood form use in the 1940s, since significantly more labor is required to create the forms for these projections than was needed in the board-form era. Capitals have nearly disappeared because of architectural concerns about space planning and difficulties in forming and reinforcing.

"Waffle slabs" are a cross between one-way joists and flat slabs. A waffle has the depth and general form of a joist floor with joists running in both directions. Usually the voids between the projecting stems are filled in at columns to create a "built-in" drop panel and in bands between columns to create beams. Waffles are built with flat formwork supporting the metal pan void forms, making them relatively cost-efficient. Waffle slabs allow high floor loads, but at the cost of a deep floor.

Another variation of the flat-slab floor is the flat-plate floor, which has a smooth underside and lacks beams, drop panels, and column capitals. While flat-plate floors typically can carry less load than flat-slab floors of similar thickness and reinforcing, they are far easier to build because the formwork required is completely flat. These floors provide the thinnest floor-plate (floor top to ceiling bottom) dimension of any structural system. High-rise apartment houses are ideally suited for flat-plate construction because the partitions between rooms provide plenty of places to hide columns and the thin floor plate allows for more levels to be packed into the given height of the building. However, the apartment layouts often force the column locations off of a regular rectangular grid. The reinforcing patterns in the slabs are therefore irregular, increasing the probability of odd cracking. It is important to identify flat slabs, and particularly flat plates, early in an investigation, as flat-slab floors are very difficult to modify (for example, cutting a hole for a staircase) because there are no members other than the slab to take stress.

Reinforced-concrete frame buildings are usually defined by the type of floor used, but there are, of course, other elements present. Columns in concrete buildings tend to be fairly large compared to steel columns. Concrete columns 2 feet square are not at all unusual, and concrete-frame high-rise office buildings can have columns 4 feet on a side. Most columns are square or rectangular in plan, although round columns are possible. Round columns are actually stronger than square columns of a similar size, but they are less frequently used because of the architectural difficulties they create. Any shape of column may be hidden behind finishes that mask the shape.

Compared to building individual columns and light partitions, erecting reinforced concrete walls is an expensive and slow process. Concrete walls can, however, serve as shear walls, providing lateral resistance to the entire building frame. Many concrete buildings derive their lateral strength from walls surrounding elevator shafts or other core elements. Since the difference between a concrete wall and gypsum-board and metal-stud partitions is obvious, the presence or absence of shear walls is one of the first determinations that can be made after a building is identified as concrete.

Unlike steel frames, there is no distinct division between members or structural systems in concrete frames. Floor slabs merge into beams, which run directly into columns with no obvious connection. There are connection details in the rebar, but they are invisible when the finished surfaces of the concrete are examined visually. Unless excessive structural movement or incorrect original design is suspected, investigation of concrete buildings rarely includes detailed investigation of the connections. Steel-framing connections can be exposed by removing finishes, while investigation from scratch of the strength of a concrete frame requires extensive probing to determine rebar sizes and locations.

4
Mechanical Systems

Unlike structural systems, which may be entirely hidden from view, the mechanical systems of a building must be visible at certain points. For example, no matter how well concealed electrical outlets may be, they must be accessible to a building's occupants or they are useless. It is therefore possible to gain a sense of the extent of wiring in a building simply by counting outlets and switches. Certain portions of mechanical systems, such as meter rooms, may provide a great deal of information about the links between the building systems and outside utilities and about the types of systems in the building. The first step in a mechanical investigation is to look at the areas of the building where the systems are exposed—for example, the crawl space or cellar of a house or the basement, vaults, or distribution closets in an office building.

Building mechanical systems have grown steadily more complex over time, and there is no reason to assume that this process has ended. Telecommunications equipment is not discussed here as it is typically part of a tenant's "furniture" and not the base building, but the trend towards "smart-building" systems may erase this distinction some day. More ordinary systems include:

- plumbing
- drainage

- gas
- electricity
- lighting
- heating
- ventilation
- air-conditioning
- sprinklers

Plumbing

A simple description of the plumbing within a building is that water enters the building from an outside source, usually a branch off a utility company's main, passes through a usage meter, divides into local branches that serve individual fixtures, reconnects into drains, and then leaves the building for an outside destination, either a public sewer or a septic system. (Figure 4-1) Secondary branches (such as the vents going up to the outside air required for each drain, roof drains, and sumps below the main drain elevation) do not affect the basic working of the system.

4-1. Modern seismic design includes mechanical equipment supports as well as base structure. The pipes in this space in a 1930 building are suspended with movement dampers, indicating they are either a recent addition or have been re-hung.

4-2. A water storage tank at the top of an 1880s building. The tank is elevated to maintain pressure at the top floor of the building. Modern tanks may be hidden, but are essentially similar.

Water supply is the only system that may be unmetered. Almost all localities now require water metering for new construction, but in well-watered areas with old, established public water supply systems, water service may have been unmetered for a long time. In such cases, including most of the large cities in the eastern half of the United States, old buildings that have not been altered may still have unmetered connections to the main. The other possible source of unmetered water is a well serving one building, but these have become steadily more rare except in the countryside.

Short buildings typically use the pressure of the water service to deliver water where it is needed. Tall buildings use pumps to deliver water directly to high floors or to a storage tank near the top of the building from which the water is gravity-fed back down. (Figure 4-2) The definition of "short" and "tall" in this case depends on the pressure available from the water supply. Pressure from water mains is usually enough to raise water three to five stories, while pressure from wells is usually only adequate for one or two.

The most important questions for the owner usually concern the type of fixtures in use and the capacity to change or add fixtures. Since the fixtures must be visible to be useful, a simple walkthrough of kitchens, bathrooms, and laundry rooms gives an accurate fixture count. Capacity is based on the capacity of the building's service and the capacity of the risers, both of which are normally visible in the basement.

Drainage

The portion of the water and waste disposal system within a building is similar in appearance and construction to the water supply system. The water supply leads from one main to distribution risers to a set of local branches serving individual fixtures, while the waste leads from the fixtures to risers to one main. (Figure 4-3) Depending on a building's location, the biggest difference may be what happens with the waste main. In

4-3. A cast-iron drain pipe. The small Y connection is not an abandoned branch, but rather a "clean-out" to permit a plumber's snake to be introduced to clean the inside of the pipe below.

cities and many suburban and exurban developments, the main leads to a public sewer located near the building (the counterpart to a public water main). The waste line from isolated buildings, particularly houses, may lead to a septic tank or septic field. These are holding areas where the waste water can evaporate and the solids decay. Septic fields are more or less self-sustaining but require large areas of land; tanks are small but occasionally need to be cleaned of the waste products. Few building investigations include thorough investigations of septic tanks or fields. Besides the obvious unpleasant aspects of the task, it is considered more a maintenance issue than a part of the permanent building condition.

Gas

Widespread commercial use of electric lighting began in the 1880s, but the system did not spread to many homes until the early twentieth century. Prior to the introduction of electric light, the majority of American homes and businesses were lit by burning gas. Since then, gas has been used extensively for kitchen equipment, heating systems, and some forms of central cooling equipment. It can be quickly determined if gas is currently installed in a kitchen by looking at the stove and oven; if the kitchen has electric (or wood-burning) equipment, assume that existing gas piping is limited to mechanical spaces.

The basic layout of a gas system resembles that of an electrical or water system. The service enters the building from a main, where service is broken up for distribution. Unlike water, gas is almost always submetered for each tenant within a building. Depending on the size of the building and the number of tenants requiring meters, the gas risers may be part of the common system, with meters located at each floor for the various branches, or the meters may be grouped together near where the main enters the building.

The gas used in the nineteenth century was "artificial gas" produced from coal, while modern systems use the natural gas found near oil deposits. Because gas is both poisonous and potentially explosive, the piping must be entirely airtight. Unlike water pipe, which uses screw joints that may leak small amounts of water with no great damage to the surrounding structure, gas pipe is always continuously soldered together. There is no way a visual survey can determine that the piping joints are tight, so any gas system that is suspect should be tested with water by a plumber.

Electricity

Portions of a building's electrical system are by nature visible, while other portions are ordinarily hidden. Meters are usually located where the service from the electric utility enters the building, occasionally on the outside of private houses and small commercial buildings, usually on the inside of other buildings. Meters, switch boxes, and circuit breakers (or in older buildings, fuse boxes) are meant to be seen by the building's occupants and so are easy to find. Maintenance of the portion of the system "outside" of the meter is the electric utility's responsibility. While this can cause difficulties when the building owner wants to change service or if there is a chronic problem with the distribution, it also means that information on this portion of the system is available from the utility's records.

Besides the basic elements such as convenience outlets and wall switches, the only user-operated electrical equipment is a circuit breaker. Circuit breakers are designed to cut off the current to an electric circuit if the demand on that circuit exceeds the capacity of the wiring. Fuses are a form of mechanical circuit breaker; the current is switched off by the melting of a small piece of metal tape inside the glass fuse body. More modern circuit breakers are spring-loaded switches that switch from "on" to "off" by themselves as they start to overheat from excessive current. Most buildings have circuit breakers near where the power enters the building and then again at various locations on branch circuits. In an apartment house, there is usually a main circuit breaker and then another in each apartment; in an office building the power distribution is often at a high voltage, and the circuit breakers are hidden in distribution closets.

An examination of an electrical system should include such basics as the capacity of the main circuit breaker and the capacity of the various circuits in the individual circuit breakers. Breakers made for use at ordinary voltage levels (110 and 220 volts in the United States) have their capacity in amperes stamped on the switch. More thorough investigations can include mapping the circuits (for example, finding out which breakers are connected to which outlets) as the first step toward recreating the electrical design drawings for the building.

In contrast to the visible portions of the electric system, the bulk of the conduit that carries electrical wiring from the main meter to local meters, local switches, distribution closets, outlets, and fixtures is hidden within partitions, above ceilings, and within floors. If there is a reason to suspect inadequate wiring or damage to the wiring or conduit, there is no choice but to probe. Older forms of conduit may not meet current code, although all but the most archaic are grandfathered and can still be used. The only inherently unsafe form of wiring once used is that of exposed copper wire running within walls and supported on porcelain spools. Because of the high possibility of fire and shock, this system fell out of use when electric power spread to homes.

Lighting

The first and still primary use of electric power in buildings is to provide lighting. Depending on the purpose of a room, lighting can be provided by windows supplemented by electric lights, by electric lights plugged into outlets, or by permanently wired electric lights. If the electric portion of an investigation has included identifying circuits and mapping outlets, the only specifically lighting-oriented work required is looking at the fixtures themselves.

The design of lighting (and therefore the detailed examination of existing lighting) is a specialized field that concentrates on providing proper light levels for a given room without wasting an excessive amount of electricity. Most investigations list the number and type of permanent fixtures without attempting to categorize the lighting system—in other words, an open office might have its lighting described as fluorescent with two bulb fixtures and plastic lenses at 8 feet on center in both directions. The quality of the light provided is not elaborated beyond general notations such as "light levels okay."

Handheld light meters quickly provide data on the actual light levels at various locations within a room. If such an investigation is being performed, it is critical to use the meter to represent the eye of an occupant: if you are trying to determine the amount of light available on a desk surface, the meter should be pointed down, at the desk, just as a person's eyes would be. Pointing the meter up (toward the lights) would give an artificially high reading.

Heating

With the exception of a small number of rural houses heated solely by wood stoves, all modern buildings located outside the tropics have heating systems to keep the building interiors at occupiable temperatures during cold weather. Heating systems also resemble the systems already described: heat is distributed around a building from a central location.

Several distinct system types have developed, and the first task in investigation is identification. The types are distinguished first by the medium used to carry heat: steam, water, or air.

A fourth type of system that is technically an air system but is significantly different in its operation is electric heat. The relatively high price of using electricity to heat large areas has kept this option to niche markets. Electric systems create heat through the resistance to current, in a similar fashion to toasters and electric ovens. This can work on the large scale required to heat a building, but it requires large amounts of electricity and has few advantages other than its elimination of the local fuel-burning boiler.

The type of heating elements visible in a room may provide identification for the heating system as a whole. Fin tubes, which are simply pipes surrounded by small squares of sheet metal, are used to heat buildings with hot-water systems. They are usually covered by decorative sheet metal and may be referred to as baseboard heating or baseboard radiators. Large, old-fashioned radiators indicate the use of a steam system. (Figure 4-4) The lack of any visible radiators usually indicates an air system.

Another water option is the fan-coil unit, which physically resembles a radiator in size (roughly 2 feet high and 3 feet long) but is easily identified by the fact that it contains a fan that blows air through a grille. A hot-water pipe passes through the unit, and the fan forces air through the unit and past fins on the pipe. Fan-coil units can be set in exterior walls to draw in outside air, combining ventilation with heating, or can be set inside rooms to draw in room air for heating and recirculation. Most forms of fan-coil units provide both heating and cooling.

The heating elements within the various rooms are the end of a system that includes some form of central heating plant and a distribution network for air, water, or steam. Over the course of the nineteenth and twentieth centuries, heating plants have developed from wood and coal burning to gas and oil burning. Boilers, like most other mechanical equipment in buildings, are not easily examined by nonexperts. However, anyone performing an investigation can determine the fuel source by the presence of a gas service and meter, oil tank, or coal bin.

In temperate climates, large-scale heating is required in the winter, but the only heating required in the summer is the creation of hot water. The use of the same boiler to create relatively small amounts of hot water is inefficient, so many buildings have a secondary system. In private houses

4-4. The pipe in the corner is a steam riser, feeding the radiator below the window. Note the peeling paint: since the building is known to have been built in the 1920s, there is a high probability that the paint contains lead.

and small commercial buildings it may be literally a hot-water heater, while in larger buildings it usually resembles a small boiler. Modern heating plants may consist of modular boilers, which are a set of small, identical units. As more heating is required, more of the units switch on. The advantages of this system are that it is generally highly efficient, maintenance can take place on some units while others are still operating, and no secondary heat source is needed to provide hot water in the summer.

Ventilation

Buildings of all sizes and types built before the 1950s have operable windows to admit fresh air. Ventilation systems in buildings built before this date usually use an air heating system (ductwork in large auditoriums, informal floor grilles in houses). The introduction of air-conditioning coupled with changing standards that emphasize outside air over recirculated air have led to a great increase in the amount of artificial (forced) ventilation.

With the widespread introduction of central air-conditioning after World War II, sealed buildings—those without operable windows—became common. The belief that mechanical ventilation could entirely replace natural ventilation changed architectural form; office buildings and stores became much larger in plan, creating windowless interior spaces with no natural ventilation. An entire generation of office buildings, department stores, and shopping malls built in the 1960s, '70s , and '80s relies on artificial ventilation for all fresh air. Many other building types in this period were also built with sealed windows, including apartment houses and hospitals, although the trend never went as far as it did with commercial structures.

There has been some backlash against sealed buildings, particularly since the discovery of issues of indoor air quality (IAQ) and sick building syndrome. Air pollution was first thought of as a problem with outside air, but testing has shown that indoor air can contain dangerously high levels of chemical toxins and biological agents (including bacteria and fungi). IAQ problems tend to be worse in sealed buildings, which have a higher level of air recirculation than traditionally vented buildings and which contain air-handling equipment that sometimes serves as breeding grounds. "Sick building syndrome" is the name given to buildings that have persistently high levels of respiratory illness among occupants. The cause is usually related to IAQ problems but may be difficult to correlate with a specific building system or material.

The central component of ventilation systems is an air handler, which provides distribution of forced air down a number of ducts. When ventilation systems are combined with the heating plant, air-conditioning, or both, the fans and duct controls that make up an air handler may be distributed within other equipment. Unlike boilers or cooling towers, which are heavy and complex heat exchangers, air handlers consist of a few simple components: fans, ducts, duct valves, and filters. Filters can provide a rough guide to the quality of maintenance of a ventilation system: they should be cleaned regularly because of the possibility of biological growth in a wet, dirty medium.

Air intakes may exist in isolation or be combined with the heating or air-conditioning equipment. In either case, fresh air is drawn in to the building, usually passes through a filter to remove particulate pollution, and then is distributed through a network of sheet-metal ducts. Like the other systems described, the network works its way down from major trunks to small branches, in this case ending in wall, ceiling, and floor grilles. Unlike with other smaller, more intricate systems, the relative importance of a section of duct is easy to identify: the final branches of ducts usually have an 8- to 16-inch cross-section, while risers can be as big as 8 feet square.

Vertical risers typically run in dedicated shafts, which may be visible only as unexplained thick partitions. Access doors to duct shafts can help in identifying these locations. Horizontal runs of duct are usually above ceilings and can be located by the line of grilles branching off. If the ductwork is left architecturally exposed, the investigation is made that much simpler.

Any building that has forced ventilation must have a method of expelling used air. Return-air ducts form a similar network to fresh air ducts, building up from relatively small branches to larger trunks. The biggest difference between the two systems is that noise is less of a concern with return-air ducts, so larger duct sizes and more direct connections from grilles to trunks can be made. The return trunks lead to a combination of outside vents and air-handling units for recirculation.

If a return-air plenum is used, it may be visible only by the absence of return ducts. In other words, spaces used for other purposes, including occupied spaces, can serve as return-air plenums. The key to identifying a plenum is that there must at some point be a connection to an air handler that expels air to the outside or feeds it back to the ventilation system for recirculation. A dead-end space without such a connection is not a plenum.

Air-conditioning

The inexact phrase "air-conditioning" almost always is used to mean cooling, although in special circumstances it can include humidification and dehumidification. Unlike heating, which can exist in isolation, air-conditioning is almost always linked to ventilation. This is in part due to the relative difficulty of cooling compared to heating: a "primitive" system of steam heat and ventilation through operable windows functions fairly well despite the heat loss from partially opened windows, while few cooling systems are powerful enough to overcome the heat gain from open windows on a hot day.

All of the other mechanical operations described here are seen in buildings as part of an overall system. Isolated, small-scale heating units (e.g., portable electric heaters), like temporary toilets (e.g., portable chemical toilets), exist, but are never considered part of the permanent building fabric. Office workers may use electric heaters under their desks if the building's heating system is inadequate, but an investigator would not describe those heaters as part of the system. Air-conditioning is the exception. Common through-the-wall and window-mounted air conditioners, are electric appliances that more closely resemble refrigerators than they do comprehensive heating systems. Central air-conditioning systems have been slowly gaining popularity in all types of buildings and are a requirement in sealed buildings that use only mechanical ventilation, but they still are not universal.

Cooling is distributed through using air or water as a medium. Ice would be the cooling system's equivalent of a heating system's steam, but that solution is not practical on a large scale. Isolated units draw in either outside or recirculated air, cool the air and blow it indoors, and expel the heat to the outside of the building. Whether air or water is used depends on a number of architectural design criteria and the other mechanical systems in use.

Even water cooling systems ultimately rely on air to cool the building interior. This is in contrast to steam radiators, which transfer heat in part though infrared radiation. The use of radiation is impractical for cooling because it would require the contents of a room, including the occupants, to radiate heat toward the cool surface since radiation always transfers from the hotter object to the cooler. The cool surface would need to be larger in area than is architecturally acceptable, and the degree of radiation from the room contents would be affected by furnishings and clothing and therefore unpredictable.

If mechanical ventilation is in use in a building, the air can be cooled as well as heated using one basic system to provide the three functions. As with air heating, air cooling requires a greater volume of air than would be required solely for ventilation requirements. The air-volume requirements for heating and cooling in temperate climates are fairly close, so there are economies of scale in using both simultaneously. The conspicuous lack of radiators and baseboard units that signal air heating is usually a good indicator of air cooling.

Water systems can usually be identified by the fan-coil units in each room. These are the same units described in the section on heating. When fan-coil units are used for cooling, they are most commonly mounted in the exterior walls to supply fresh air. If the units do not have direct fresh-air sources, there will be fresh-air ducts serving each room in addition to the cold water.

The cooling equivalent of a boiler is a cooling tower or heat exchanger.

These pieces of equipment are the center of cooling systems and cool the distribution air or water by expelling the excess heat into the outside air. Most large buildings have cooling towers that rest on dunnage above the roof and have fans blowing hot, moist air up; smaller buildings tend to have smaller, split heat exchangers that sit directly on the roof.

The process of cooling air in many climates automatically induces some degree of dehumidification. Hot air has a greater capacity to carry water vapor than cold air, so if humid, hot air is cooled, the water vapor will condense. Because cooled air is less humid than hot air, air-conditioning systems do not often explicitly include dehumidification. This is also the reason that air conditioners of all types tend to drip water. The vapor condenses on cold surfaces, and the coldest surfaces in an air conditioner are the refrigerant coils. Once the water has condensed on the surface, it collects into larger droplets and then drips off. Small wall units usually have a built-in drip pan and drain leading to the outside of the building, while large cooling towers and internal cooling coils have separate drip pans mounted below. In either case, corroded, bent, or leaking drip pans can cause staining and damage to finishes. Drip pans below large pieces of air-conditioning equipment have also been shown to be prime sources of fungi and other biological air pollutants.

Sprinklers

The idea of having a system to distribute water within a building to put out fires dates back to the nineteenth century. Ordinary sprinkler systems, where distribution pipes that are always full of water run through ceilings or in the occupied spaces, have been used longest in factories, are now required in most types of commercial buildings, and are becoming a requirement in more types and more locations within apartment houses. They can be used in private homes but are not required by code and are rarely installed.

Besides the distribution pipe, which resembles ordinary plumbing, the components of a system are a storage tank (usually separate from the other water system) and the heads that deliver water. The heads resemble the heads for lawn sprinklers, since they must also take water from a stream and distribute it evenly around a large area. (Figure 4-5) The most basic type of head is restrained from spraying water by a small metal fuse with a low melting point. When a fire starts, heat quickly builds up below the ceiling, melting the fuse and triggering the spray.

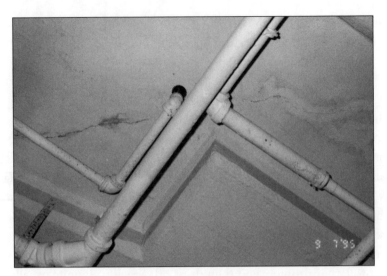

4-5. Exposed plumbing in a warehouse: a local sprinkler branch is on the left with a head at the center; a main drain pipe runs upper right to lower left; a main sprinkler branch is on the right.

Ordinary sprinkler systems are easy to identify, as the sprinkler heads are visible even if the piping is not. The heads project down through ceilings or sideways through walls near the ceilings at regular intervals, with at least one head per room. Areas with decorative ceilings may have a type of head that is hidden within the ceiling but drops into the room when triggered to spray. These hidden heads are more difficult to find but are still visible as flat disks roughly 3 inches in diameter.

There are two main objections to the use of sprinklers. The first is aesthetic—some consider sprinkler heads unattractive—and is addressed by using hidden heads. The second is that the water damages interior finishes and building contents. When compared with fire damage, sprinklers are obviously the lesser of two evils, but they are inappropriate for some historic buildings and museums.

Special Systems

Steam systems
In heavily built-up portions of cities, steam may be provided by utility companies in the same manner as electricity and water. Steam mains run under streets and have meter branches feeding to buildings. This service eliminates individual buildings' need for furnaces, although they do need

a heat exchanger to transfer the heat from the steam to the building's hot water supply. Most of the equipment within the building is identical to that used with a local boiler. Large campuses, such as hospitals or colleges, may have a central boiler with a similar set of steam mains serving individual buildings.

Elevators and escalators

Elevators and escalators are specialized equipment that can only be properly investigated, maintained, and repaired by experts. Buildings themselves are basically immobile, and most mechanical building systems consist largely of a network of interchangeable and simple elements (pipe, duct, conduit). In contrast, elevators and escalators are tightly integrated and precise machines. A good example of the fundamental difference between buildings and machines is construction tolerance: most structural elements have an allowed tolerance for incorrect sizing in the range of ¼ to ½ inch, and the tolerance for mislocation of hidden ductwork may be as high as 2 or 3 inches, but mistakes as small as ⅒ inch can disrupt elevator operation. Ordinary investigation addresses elevators when determining the construction and support of the shaft and the floor openings. In most frame buildings, the shaft is built of concrete block or gypsum board and metal studs supported at each floor, while in bearing-wall buildings the shafts may be structural and supporting the floors.

Alarms

Fire and security alarms are also specialized systems that can only be properly evaluated by experts. The systems cannot be evaluated by observation (although observation will reveal if the equipment is physically damaged) but only by testing the sensors, control panels, and remote alarms. (Figure 4-6) Because these systems are sensitive to the use and internal layout of the building, they are often changed by new owners or tenants. Investigators have to be particularly careful about alarmed doors and windows. Since most investigations require walking through every part of a building, including rarely visited locations such as unoccupied roofs and fire stairs, triggering alarms is unfortunately common.

Oil tanks

Buried oil tanks on site are not explicitly part of the building condition but can be expensive to deal with. Such tanks are part of an oil-heating sys-

4-6. A new fire alarm system (the box and associated wiring) and new electric wiring in conduit are more visible in this storage space than is ordinarily found in finished spaces.

tem. During the course of the last half of the twentieth century, the standards for protection of tanks against weathering and for containment of oil leaks have become much more strict. Modern regulations require that the tanks not be directly buried but rather located inside the building in a containment room, or in a buried vault. The federal Environmental Protection Agency (EPA), state environmental agencies, and local governments all have regulations about buried tanks: when they must be removed, how they must be treated if they are to be abandoned in place, and how potentially contaminated soil must be treated. A document search and physical investigation for buried tanks should be conducted if any excavation is to take place, if there is any reason to believe that there may be abandoned tanks on the property or in the cellar, or if there are any outstanding environmental violations. Actually removing or treating tanks is a specialized field for consultants and contractors who know all of the regulations regarding safe disposal of contaminated material.

5
Damage

Many investigations are ultimately about damage. If all buildings were known to be in good condition, there would be little reason to examine them. Even investigation performed for other reasons, such as feasibility studies for alteration, often hinge on the condition of the existing structure. (Figure 5-1) Inspectors not investigating damage may still find it, in which case the damage must be documented and, usually, repaired.

Structural Failure Mechanisms

To understand structural behavior, you must understand how structures fail. Examining the condition of an existing building is much easier if a similar building has recently collapsed. When such a resource is not available, investigators must look for signs of the beginning of failure.

Investigation is a skill that obviously improves with practice. The more buildings an individual examines, the more types of actual and incipient failure that person will see. The best way to learn to read damage is to look for it in every building, regardless of the reason the building is being examined. This includes looking for damage in areas where it might not be expected.

The signs that appear when damage first takes place—the first cracks in a masonry wall or the first movement of a floor—are more indicative of

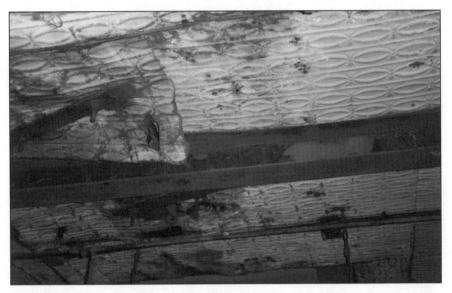

5-1. The tin ceiling is heavily rusted, suggesting long-term water leakage that may have damaged the wood joists above.

the type of material and the type of damage than of the severity of the damage. Since severity can be easily judged, a combination of examining signs of failure with an examination of the overall severity of the damage gives enough information to begin the design of repairs.

Investigation Theory

Physical damage can be attributed to one of three basic causes: material deterioration from chemical or mechanical action, overstress from load, and overstress from excessive movement (also referred to as secondary stress). However, it is not possible to look only for deterioration and overstress when looking for damage, because deterioration may be hidden and overstress itself is not visible. These causes must be determined on the basis of their symptoms: cracking and buckling from overstress, and oxidation, delamination, softening, and biological growth from material deterioration.

No one (except possibly an engineer directly involved in investigation) actually cares about the level of stress within a structural member, or even the exact amount of damage that may be present. What most people feel is important is the conclusion of the structural investigation—the statement concerning the safety (or lack of safety) of the building. Obviously, examination of specifics is the only way to collect the information needed to reach a conclusion, but the specifics can be misleading. For example, a building can have numerous cracks in masonry bearing walls, sloping joist floors, and water-damaged mortar in its foundation walls and still be safe for use. Conversely, a building with no obvious signs of damage may have hidden weathering that has greatly reduced its ability to carry load. Examination that focuses on the specifics can give a misleading impression of the overall condition. The key to understanding the actual conditions is to look for patterns of damage. A single crack in a masonry wall could have many explanations, but a pattern of diagonal cracks spreading down and to the side of the corners of window heads strongly suggests one or two types of problems associated with the lintels.

It is not possible to determine the state of stress within a structural member simply through observation. Even using advanced nondestructive testing techniques, determining the likelihood of failure for a steel beam can be difficult and extremely expensive. Some structures, such as wood floor joists, show substantial movement under ordinary and acceptable loads, providing a simple indicator of stress. Most structures, including brick walls, and steel or concrete beams and columns are opaque to examination; unless they are obviously damaged, careful investigation is required to find potential failure. The effect of structural movements on adjacent nonstructural elements can, however, be a useful secondary source of information on the condition of the structure itself.

One of the best tools available in examining a structure is the disparity between stiffness and strength. This difference, which may seem merely a game of semantics (since everyone wants buildings that are both strong and resistant to movement), is crucial to understanding the action of any material. A material's strength lies in its ability to withstand a specific level of stress; stiffness is gauged by the amount of deflection caused by a given amount of stress. Many structures are quite stiff at first (that is, until they fail) but are not particularly strong. A good example is a sheet of paper: it is quite stiff when loaded in plane, as is demonstrated if you try to pull it out of square. It is not, however particularly strong.

The analogy of a sheet of paper to building structure is not far-fetched. Brick curtain walls, which were very popular from the 1890s until the 1940s and are still common today, are enormously stiff when loaded in plane, but are incapable of withstanding the structural loads placed on them by their own stiffness. Wind blowing on a brick curtain wall building is properly resisted by the building's frame, which is either steel or concrete. If the brick is not provided with expansion joints, however, the exterior walls parallel to the direction of the wind are stiffer than the internal frame, and therefore will start to carry a substantial portion of the lateral wind load. Unlike the frame, the walls are quickly over-stressed and will crack. The cracks reduce their stiffness, and their proportion of the load is reduced. The longer the walls resist lateral load, the more they crack, which reduces their ability to resist lateral load. Buildings with proper expansion joints do not develop these cracks, as the relatively small, mutually isolated areas of wall created by the joints are not stiff enough to resist any substantial portion of the lateral load.

The examination of exterior walls for cracks is a well-known part of building investigation, but the same technique provides clues about many different structural conditions. (Figure 5-2) The ideal indicator of build-

5-2. The "crack" on the side wall of the building, starting to the left of the cornice and running down at least as far as the chimney's shadow, is not a structural crack. It is an original design flaw where the brick of the front and side walls was never properly joined. It is potentially as dangerous as a crack if, and only if, there is evidence of the walls moving apart. An actual crack in this location would indicate that the walls were moving strongly enough to pull bricks apart. (Note that the modern chimney is abandoned and in pieces, and there is an abandoned masonry flue built into and projecting from the wall.)

ing movement is a nonstructural member that is very stiff, extremely weak, and visible during a cursory examination. This indicator exists in many old buildings in the form of plaster-covered partitions. Modern gypsum-board partitions are not as useful because they tend to split at the joints rather than where the stress is, but they are still useful. Partitions in older masonry-bearing-wall buildings with wood-joist floors are typically wood stud and lath covered with plaster. Partitions in older frame buildings are typically gypsum block or terra-cotta tile covered with plaster. Plaster, gypsum block, and terra cotta are ideal materials for the purposes of investigation, since they are very brittle and weak in tension but when assembled into partitions are nearly as stiff as a brick wall.

Various material properties also provide useful information. Simply put, certain materials have unique properties that explain common modes of failure. An observer noting one of those failures should look for the material in question as the most likely explanation. Three examples are: wetting expansion of terra cotta, delamination of steel during corrosion, and cracking of reinforced concrete under load. The first is a peculiarity of terra cotta when compared with other masonry materials: kiln-dried terra cotta expands when wet but does not recover the full amount during drying. Terra-cotta blocks used in the past for curtain walls and interior partitions tend to grow over time if exposed to water. The most important effect of this growth is the steady increase in pressure within terra-cotta curtain walls. Since all curtain walls leak, water will reach the unglazed rear and sides of the terra cotta. The increased pressures can exceed the allowable amount for the terra cotta and, more importantly, exacerbate any other mechanisms for cracking that may be present. Knowing this property of the material can explain a pattern of pressure cracks and spalling that might otherwise be attributed to a structural cause; the pressure intensifies cracks or bulges that might be present from some of the mechanisms described below.

One of the most telling material properties in investigation is the expansion of steel as it rusts. Not only is iron oxide a less dense material than steel, but as steel rusts, the outermost layer flakes off. This process, known as delamination, causes a great expansion in the metal's volume. Rusting steel embedded in masonry or concrete pushes the encasement outward, a mechanism referred to as "rust jacking." While rust jacking is not pleasant if it is destroying your building, it is of great help in locating damaged steel. Spalls in concrete slabs at damaged rebar and bulges in

5-3. The top of a 1910s concrete foundation wall losing cohesion between the cement and the aggregate. This can be a sign of impurities in the original materials, environmental attack, or both.

brick walls at damaged spandrel beams are much easier to locate than the hidden damage to the steel.

Reinforced concrete beams and slabs crack under load. This is normal, and is accounted for in the design—if the concrete did not crack in tension, very little load would ever get transferred to the reinforcing rods. By examining the cracks in a reinforced concrete structure, the location of the tension areas of continuous beams and slabs can be located. Again, the material property in question reveals information about loads and movement that would be otherwise hidden. (Figure 5-3)

Investigation Examples

As mentioned above, rust jacking can provide information about hidden damage to masonry curtain walls. Many older buildings were built without any waterproofing on the spandrel beams and columns, relying instead on the brick to protect the steel. Newer buildings, while providing some type of water protection, often have expansion joints located at the columns and beams, where water can cause damage if the joints are not maintained. In concrete-frame buildings where the slab cantilevers past the exterior columns to carry the curtain wall, the exposed edge of concrete is vulnerable to water.

The common pattern of damage from rusting steel spandrel beams include horizontal outward bulges in the brick that repeat at each floor level, particularly when accompanied by cracks. Rusting spandrel columns can cause similar vertical bulges and cracks, although vertical cracks can be caused by other mechanisms and should not be taken as proof of steel damage. The damage is often concentrated at changes in the facade that may collect or direct water, so the outward displacement of a precast string course located near a spandrel beam in an otherwise undamaged brick wall fits the prevailing pattern.

A similar pattern that appears in bearing-wall buildings is a series of small vertical cracks at each floor level, spaced at regular intervals of 6 to 10 feet along the length of the building. This is usually indicative of rusting of the bearing ends of floor beams. Since the beams are spaced regularly, their ends, when rusting, create the visible pattern of cracks. This pattern is composed of a series of points of damage rather than the continuous bulges and cracks in the curtain wall patterns described earlier. This difference can provide information about a building's unknown structure during the first minutes of an investigation. (Figure 5-4)

Cracks that run nearly the full height of the building and are concentrated near exterior corners are usually indicators of building movement, not material damage, although the two causes may be related. Thermal expansion of unrelieved walls and stresses caused by the walls' resistance to lateral load (described earlier) are the major causes of cracks at the exterior corners of masonry-curtain-wall buildings. Once the cracks are formed, water may enter and cause steel damage that increases the size of the cracks, but the pattern of long vertical cracks should be seen as an indicator of building movement and wall construction, not necessarily steel damage.

Another pattern that indicates a structural cause for nonstructural damage is the appearance of compression failure in curtain walls on concrete frames. Concrete frames have substantially more column shortening, including long-term creep, than steel frames. If the curtain walls are erected shortly after the concrete is placed (a common practice) and an adequate amount of space for shortening is not provided at each floor, the curtain wall will be compressed and suffer damage similar to that of the terra-cotta curtain walls described previously.

5-4. A series of beams formerly embedded in a masonry wall and resting on a steel grillage beam below. The beam ends are heavily rusted, with holes entirely through the webs.

The requirements for reinforcing concrete have changed over the years. Older concrete designs may have significantly less top (continuity) rebar than the current standards. As a result, it is common to see parallel cracks in the top of concrete slabs in older buildings, regardless of whether they are steel frame or concrete frame. The concrete over the tops of the beams is in tension from "negative moment" bending, as opposed to the better-known condition of tension at the center of the bottom of a slab span. The cracks are, by themselves, not indicators of any damage other than the cracking previously described as a normal feature of concrete design, but when present with a source of water (e.g., the slabs at any roof, or those in a garage), they may represent areas where the rebar and beams below are damaged. Cracks or spalls in areas known to be in compression, such as the middle of the top surface of one-way slab spans, are an indication of more serious problems, usually rusting of the rebar. (Figure 5-5)

Repair

Repair of damage from overstress or weathering is a broad topic that cannot be easily categorized. This topic is also rarely addressed in isolation, since large-scale repairs often take place during other work like alterations or restoration. Repair design, like any other design, should only be performed by trained professionals, as an incorrect repair may cause more damage than no repair at all. Several general principles can be described, based on the same logic used to describe the patterns of damage to structural types.

If the damage has a traceable and provable cause, the cause should be directly addressed. For example, wall cracks from lack of expansion joints should be addressed by providing joints. Other damage, including the cracks that drew attention to the problem in the first place and any internal problems (such as damaged wall ties) will also need repair, but the general approach is to first address the basic cause.

If damage is the result of changes in the overall condition of a building, the past performance of the structure cannot be taken as a guide to the severity of the problem. For example, demolition of an adjoining structure may expose a wall that was never before exposed to weathering and

5-5. A garage floor with numerous concrete spalls associated with exposed and rusting reinforcing. A contractor has moved the loose pieces of concrete, exposing the full amount of spalling.

was built blind—that is, built up against the wall now demolished and therefore not finished on one face. Walls of this type typically leak a great deal, and if not protected after the demolition with parging or other waterproofing will quickly show some of the damage described earlier. The fact that no damage had been seen previously at the wall is meaningless because of the changed circumstances.

Finally, design of repairs should not proceed until the patterns of damage are identified. If cracks in the top of an otherwise adequate slab are the result of inadequate reinforcing, an extensive campaign of crack repair is pointless. The next time the slabs are loaded, the cracks will reappear in the patching material. If the damage pattern is known, the solution (leaving the cracks alone) is known as well. This is true of more complex problems, although the solutions that come straight from a pattern analysis may be more schematic than realistic, requiring several iterations of design development for actual use.

Unrelated Damage

Sometimes investigation will uncover problems that have no connection with the project. If, for example, an unsafe facade condition caused by deterioration of the ties that connect the masonry to the spandrel beams is discovered during an investigation preceding interior renovation, the designer has a responsibility to bring attention to the situation. On the other hand, just because a condition is discovered does not mean that the designer has to assume responsibility for repairing it. The proper course of action is to notify the building owner or any others responsible, such as a real estate managing agent. The investigator should state the nature and seriousness of the condition, the need for further investigation, and any remedial action required. This same report should be made if the condition appears to be immediately life threatening, but with the seriousness emphasized and the suggestion of an immediate course of action to ameliorate the danger. This can include shoring, the construction of protection such as sidewalk bridges, or evacuation of a portion or all of the building. After being notified of the nature and severity of the problem, the building's representative will decide if the investigator will have further involvement in the issue at hand.

6
Documentation

$\mathbf{A}$nyone working on an existing building is part of a series of people (including architects, engineers, contractors, occupants, and owners) who have passed through the building. In most cases, some of the previous people have examined (or designed), thought about, and documented the building. In all cases (other than buildings slated for demolition) it is safe to assume that more people will be examining the building in the future. This determines much of the strategy in using drawings and reports.

Original documentation that may be of interest includes:

- original design drawings
- original shop drawings
- drawings from alterations
- drawings from previous investigations
- reports from previous investigations
- original construction photographs
- photographs or videos from previous investigations

Reading Original Drawings

The most obvious source of information—original design or construction drawings—is also the easiest to use. While the level of detail on old drawings varies widely and rarely is extensive enough to answer all potential questions, the drawings are the result of a design process that is essentially the same as the one we use today. Often, ninety-year-old design drawings are no more difficult for a designer to read than are any drawings produced by someone else. In some cases, old drawings actually contain more information on a given topic than do their modern counterparts. Loose lintels, for example, were regularly shown on floor plans as late as the 1930s, while on modern drawings lintel sizes are usually buried in a general note or, worse, in a specification thrown away after construction.

Not everyone is expert at reading drawings, and the physical deterioration of old drawings, particularly when printed with white lines on a blue background, only increases the difficulty. Unless a note is unmistakably clear (the notation "2x4 @ 16," which means that wood studs are nominally 2 inches by 4 inches in section and spaced at 16 inches on center, has appeared on drawings in the same form since at least the 1880s), the information must be studied before it is used. When an ambiguous or obscure note is deciphered, a clear note in modern notation should be made on a copy of the drawing.

There are more similarities than differences between old and new drawings. A floor plan will almost always show dimensions to any grid or column lines used, beam sizes in a steel frame, the location of floor openings, and the perimeter building lines. Old drawings have a tendency to show all masonry walls, even curtain walls, at equal weight as steel or concrete structure. This is probably a historically intriguing carryover from the days of masonry-bearing-wall buildings, but it is an enormous nuisance in reading the drawings. A single heavy line is usually a beam, but a pair of heavy lines can stand for a masonry wall, a concrete beam, or, in the era before large rolled steel beams, a pair of beams acting in tandem as a girder. Since all three of these possibilities are realistic floor supports, and since before 1920, buildings often had mixed structural systems, the possibility for true confusion arises.

The example above shows a common problem: changes over time in design and construction standards have orphaned certain types of notation. Double beams were common before 1900 and, while gradually decreasing in popularity, were still a standard as late as 1920. People creating drawings before 1940 could assume that anyone reading the drawings would be familiar with the use of double beams and the associated details. Someone reading those same drawings fifty years later may never have heard of the obsolete practice of using double beams and is therefore more likely to misinterpret the drawings.

One of the serious problems in reading old drawings is very basic: actually reading the information provided. The standard drafting alphabet taught before World War I was more ornate than those taught today, and it usually was italicized. The combination of small, ornate, and slanted lettering and slightly different terminology can easily cause confusion. When dealing with dimension strings, the assumed reading can be verified by scaling the drawing, but for notes and beam sizes there is no solution other than to check the readings several times. Another destructive aspect of time is the physical aging of the drawings. Ink-on-cloth originals hold up well when stored out of sunlight, but even an optimist would not expect to find original, reproducible drawings on a building more than twenty years old. Old paper prints, just like new paper prints, are extremely fragile and subject to fading, cracking, tearing, and careless people's scribbling. Anyone using original prints has the responsibility to protect them. If the project budget allows it, the safest course of action is to have new, reproducible drawings photographically made from the prints, so that new prints can be used for the work while the old ones are archived. A less expensive course that creates a reasonably permanent record is to microfilm the drawings.

Beyond difficulties in physically reading the drawings, many people have difficulty in understanding the technical language. Architecture and engineering have their own jargon, which has gradually changed over time. As with most jargons, it is at its worst when abbreviated. Common abbreviations include "n.s." and "f.s." for near side and far side, "o.h." for opposite hand, "el." to mean elevation, "elev." to mean elevator, and "sim." to mean similar. These abbreviations can be confusing, especially with unfamiliar terms; for instance "o.h." can also mean "overhead," and "el." and "elev." are sometimes transposed. As with full descriptions, abbreviations change over time, so the shorthand used on an old drawing may include such relatively obscure marks as "a.t.c." for architectural terra cotta or "ditto" when a series of steel beams all are the same size. An extreme in obscure drawing notation can be seen on structural plans of steel buildings made before 1920, when the first of a series of identical beams would be marked with the size (e.g. "10I20"), the second with "ditto" and the remainder with a double quote, which served as an abbreviation of the abbreviation.

Material designations as well as descriptive language tend to change with time. When reading a drawing for a steel-frame building, sources such as American Institute of Steel Construction's "Iron and Steel Beams, 1873–1952" should be used and exact matches for beam names located. People familiar with modern beam sizes, such as W12x14, may not recognize the same beam when it is called by its original name, Junior Beam 12x4. Concrete data are more complicated, since true standardization of information was not established until the 1920s. Beam and column sizes can be shown on plan, in sections, or in schedules; reinforcing rod sizes can be shown in the same places, and patented reinforcing systems or odd-sized bars may have been used. The various methods were often thrown together on a single set of drawings. The use of schedules for beam and slab data is a relatively recent development; before World War II many projects would have beam widths dimensioned in plan, depths and longitudinal bars in section, and stirrups in beam side elevations, which were often combined with floor slab sections showing the floor's depth and reinforcing. The possible combinations of data location are endless; thus, all drawings, even those made recently, should be examined for any missing information. Old drawings tend to be collected and stored together, so examining all of the surviving drawings for a building may not be very onerous—it may simply involve looking through all of the drawings in one or two rolls.

Another flaw in old drawings is that they are time specific. Most available drawings are either original design drawings that don't reflect changes made later or alteration drawings with incomplete information about the original design. Drawings should always be marked with a date —of course, "should" does not always mean that they are. In addition to the careless marking of drawings, the date is usually written in the title block, most often in the lower right-hand corner of the drawing. Unfortunately, the corners are highly vulnerable, leaving many drawings without the dates they originally had. No matter how complete a drawing may seem, the information to be used should be verified on site as thoroughly as possible, in case the drawing was not a final rendering. During the design of a building, dozens of sets of similar but distinguishably different drawings may be produced as the design advances. There is no guarantee that the drawings that survive and are found during investigation will be the last set, and there is no guarantee that the most recent set of design drawings accurately represents the on-site conditions. Many professional design contracts require that, at the end of construction, the designers submit to the owner a set of final drawings showing as-built conditions, including any modifications made during the course of construction. These drawings are, of course, the best possible discovery during a document search.

Drawings found during research may be a subcontractor's shop drawings. In many cases, owners and contractors saved steel erection plans as as-built drawings. With the exception of possibly confusing notation, the erection plans are often more complete than the contract documents that they represent. Since erection drawings are meant to be read on construction sites and show actual member dimensions in addition to column line dimensions, they are generally less schematic than design drawings. Depending on when a given set of erection plans was produced and the type of members represented, the actual sizes may not be shown. The types of designations vary from the member sizes, to a series of consecutive numbers, to obscure codes representing the detail sheet number and information. If the designations are anything other than the member sizes, the drawings may need to be supplemented by probing to determine sizes, since key and index drawings are the least likely drawings to be saved.

Drawings produced years after the building's construction often contain much meaningful information. Other design professionals who, for a different alteration, hacked away at the same problems in investigation twenty years earlier, may have had the foresight to include their findings on their drawings. Many older buildings that no longer have original drawings do have records of repairs and alterations, creating a library that grows more complete over time. The drawings found in such a collection, or in building department files, are likely to be modern in layout and scope and have only one serious failing: they cannot be entirely trusted. Information gathered in investigations may not be accurate, and if the investigation was performed by someone not under the direction of the designer, it cannot be assumed dependable. Just as the information in original drawings requires confirmation, any information originating with previous alteration drawings should be checked in some fashion.

Obtaining Original Drawings

As useful as original drawings can be, they are often difficult to find. Once an investigation begins, the search for records begins. The files of building owners and managers should be examined for any pertinent drawings. Since they are not usually found at these locations, other sources must be consulted. Local building departments are unfortunately notorious for not preserving record copies of filed plans. This is in part because of the constant abuse of drawings being removed and replaced by people performing renovations.

The more prominent the building (because of its architecture, use, or owner) the more likely original drawings will have been saved. It is worth the effort in any investigation to find out if original drawings are readily available. If they are not, the cost of a thorough document search, including local building departments and archives, must be weighed against the amount of useful information expected to be retrieved. While it would be pleasant to believe that architectural archives save engineering drawings, it is rarely true. On the other hand, architectural information may incidentally be shown on structural or mechanical drawings and structural information may be shown on architectural drawings. Not only should all drawing types be saved; all available should be examined.

Original designers save their drawings and often provide copies for a nominal storage and reproduction fee. There can be complications if they feel that they should have been hired to perform the investigation or if the investigation concerns construction flaws. In cases where buildings are investigated for damage shortly after construction, there may be lawsuits involving the designers, or similar reasons why their help in the investigation is not available.

Old Reports and Other Written Documentation

Like old drawings, old reports may mislead, but can be useful because they represent a summary of a professional's investigation of some aspect of the building. Well-written reports contain specific information regarding the date of investigation and the exact location of conditions noted, making them relatively precise sources of information. Reports are generally hard to find unless the building has had the same owner or manager for a long period of time: architectural and engineering drawings are often kept because they seem important to nonprofessionals, while reports may seem like just more pieces of paper and be thrown out when files are cleaned. On the other hand, damaged drawings may be thrown out while reports are securely filed in an architect's, engineer's, or manager's office.

Also like old drawings, old reports may contain archaic or confusing language. In general, though, because drawings are concise summaries while reports are fuller explanations, reports are easier to read. Reports are also far more likely to have been written with a general audience in mind and often contain detailed explanations of terms used. When read by a nonprofessional, these explanations clarify the ideas; when read by a professional, they show the experience and biases of the writer.

Old Photographs and Pictures

Old photographs suffer from the same problems old drawings do, with few of the benefits drawings have. Prints are fragile and subject to deterioration, and negatives are often missing. Photos represent literally only a moment in time, and therefore cannot accurately capture changes over time unless they are part of a series of related images. The worst flaw with photos is that, before the widespread use of cameras that date-stamped pictures in the 1980s, prints are often undateable. If the date cannot be determined, any signs of damage or views of repair cannot be used in assessing current conditions. Also, undated photographs may show conditions before a past alteration. Dates for exterior photos can sometimes be determined by scrutinizing car models seen in the street or, less frequently, by noting changes in architecture, such as the presence of buildings with known construction or demolition dates. As with any source of information that has an indefinite date, photos are best used to supplement better documentation and direct field evidence.

The most useful photographs are those taken during construction by the owner or contractor and those taken during a previous investigation. Construction photographs typically are marked with the date and are taken from the same location at a set interval (e.g., once each week). They are more reliable than pictures taken by outside parties (including the designers) during construction because they show the sequence of events.

Old reports may have accompanying photos, but they are often photocopied and therefore hard to read. It is possible, although not likely, that old reports may mislabel photographs for location and time, reducing the value of someone else's illustrated report.

More recently, video or film records may have been created by someone else investigating the building. Still photographs from any source may be useful if their dates and locations can be determined, but films and videos not specifically made to illustrate building issues are often useless.

The useful information in an investigation has to do with details, and it is unlikely that a video made of a building will show those details. Occasionally, videos are made to illustrate issues about a building as part of the preparation for litigation. Videos of this type often specifically highlight the information that is needed.

Creating Field Drawings

Drawings created to document an investigation will range from showing the entire site to showing details at a large scale. The first drawing created (if it is not available from another source) should be a map of the site, showing the building's plan outline in relation to adjacent landmarks such as streets or other buildings. The map does not have to be to scale or even particularly accurate. Its purpose is to locate the more detailed drawings (plans, elevations, sections) that will be created later in the process. Besides the building outline, critical data for the map includes a north arrow and a rough idea of the lot boundaries.

The drawings created in an investigation are roughly the same drawings that are used to document new construction. Plans show the layout of each floor, elevations show exterior walls and interior walls of interest, sections show wall construction and relate different portions of different floors, and details show small-scale aspects of the building. (Figure 6-1)

Field drawings have to accurately distinguish between known fact and supposition. One easy way to make this distinction is through the type of dimension used, with 16'-0" used for a dimension that has been measured as 16 feet exactly, and +/- 16' or simply 16' used for a dimension that has been roughly measured or estimated at sixteen feet.

Notes taken should reflect the information important to the material or element in question. Wood member sizes should be measured and noted in actual inches (1⅝" x 3⅝") rather than nominal sizes (2x4). Steel sizes should include the member type (C, W, I, L) and as many individual measurements as can be obtained. Since web thicknesses are not usually directly obtainable, a common measurement of an old W section would be 10⅛"W, bf = 6¼", tf = ¼", for a nominal 10-inch-deep beam with flanges ¼ inch deep and 6¼ inches wide. Masonry should be noted for unit and mortar materials, surface texture, jointing, surface dimensions, type of bond if applicable, and thickness. The most important information about reinforced concrete—the size and layout of reinforcing—is not visible at all in ordinary field investigation (except through the occasional

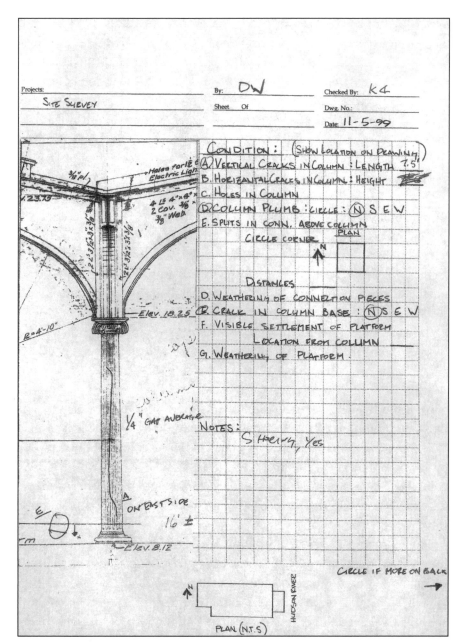

Projects: **SITE SURVEY**

By: **DW**   Checked By: **K4**

Sheet   Of

Dwg. No.:

Date: **11-5-99**

CONDITION: (SHOW LOCATION ON DRAWING)

A. VERTICAL CRACKS IN COLUMN : LENGTH 7.5'

B. HORIZONTAL CRACKS IN COLUMN : HEIGHT

C. HOLES IN COLUMN

D. COLUMN PLUMB : CIRCLE : (N) S E W

E. SPLITS IN CONN. ABOVE COLUMN

CIRCLE CORNER   PLAN

DISTANCES

D. WEATHERING OF CONNECTION PIECES

C. CRACK IN COLUMN BASE : (N) S E W

F. VISIBLE SETTLEMENT OF PLATFORM

LOCATION FROM COLUMN

G. WEATHERING OF PLATFORM

NOTES: SPALLING, YES

A ON EAST SIDE

16' ±

CIRCLE IF MORE ON BACK

PLAN (N.T.S)

HUDSON RIVER

6-1. One page of 300 identifying damage at columns in a large building. The investigator simply circled the appropriate comment for later tabulation.

spall or probe hole), limiting ordinary techniques to collecting geometric data such as the exterior dimensions of columns, the width and depth below slab underside of beams and girders, and slab thicknesses. If damage has occurred, it may be possible to see some of the rebar, in which case the size and number should be noted, and even to pick up a piece of the concrete, in which case the type of aggregate (normal weight or light weight) can be identified. Nonstructural materials should be noted in generic but detailed terms: 3" gypsum block partition rather than Pyrobar partition. Many materials first appeared as patented and available only from one manufacturer but later became generic. Many materials advanced from somewhat useful incarnations (2' x 2' plywood squares) and then plateaued in a modern form (4' x 8' sheets). The interaction of various materials may help date and identify elements: e.g., reinforced stone concrete, formed with 2' plywood squares. Estimated 1950s construction.

Incidental information that may help identify members should be noted with the member size. Several steel mills rolled their names into the webs of beams, and since knowing the manufacturer helps to identify the specific section, the name "Bethlehem" in raised letters on a piece of steel is not trivial and should be noted.

Taking Photographs

Even if the final product is an unillustrated report or a set of new design drawings, photographs taken during an investigation are extremely useful. They provide an aid to memory, so that questions concerning the report or investigation can be accurately answered long after the investigation is complete. Many modern still and video cameras automatically create date and time stamps on the pictures, creating better records of conditions at the time of specific examinations.

Photos should be taken at all locations where useful information was found, documenting it as well as possible given the inherent limitations of photography: two-dimensional representation with a limited angle of view. The location of photographs should be identified in the field notes, so that it is possible to correlate conditions in the photos with the conditions otherwise noted. The simplest way to do this is to draw an arrow with the photograph's negative number on the plan, thus providing the direction that the camera was pointed when the photograph was taken. Photographs can be incorporated into field drawings, but this is not usually done unless the field drawings are going to serve as the basis for new work.

The on-site conditions are often not conducive to quality photography. Buildings not in active use may not have interior lights; buildings undergoing construction work may be full of dust; building exteriors may not be lit from the correct direction; there may not be enough room to get the proper angle to frame the desired portion of the building. Since there is no way to improve the conditions, the investigator should take several photos and vary the camera settings to better the chances that at least one of the pictures will be clear.

Both film and digital cameras can be used, although at the time of this writing, digital cameras capable of taking pictures of the same quality as an ordinary 35mm camera cost several thousand dollars and are not ordinarily used for investigation work. Lower-resolution digital cameras are often used for general pictures in an investigation, while detailed pictures are taken with film.

The film used should reflect the detail desired in the pictures. Mid-speed color film produces the most realistic-looking photographs. Black-and-white film has relatively fine grain, providing more detail at the expense of color information and a sense of realism.

Creating Field Reports

Just as the main point of creating new field drawings is to accurately represent the conditions found in such a way as to avoid the known pitfalls of design drawings, the main point of writing a field report is to describe the conditions as accurately as possible, so that a reader who has not seen the building will understand the basic information. Reports are more often used to describe damage or abnormal conditions than ordinary circumstances and they often are accompanied by drawings or photographs showing the base conditions.

A critical element of report writing is to identify the locations of all conditions in three dimensions, measured from portions of structure unlikely to change, such as elevator shafts and structural columns: "The hole in the second floor measures +/-4' square, with its east edge +/-10' west of the east facade inside face and its north edge +/-6" south of the centerline of the northernmost column line." The three-dimensional location should be given at the beginning of the description of each condition and item noted.

While it may seem obvious that the information obtained must be presented in the report, the manner of presentation may be nearly as important as the information. The first time technical language is used, it should be spelled out in full, with abbreviations given in parentheses: "A live load of 100 pounds per square foot (psf)." This type of technical writing may be boring to read, but it avoids the worst pitfalls of jargon.

Exact member information should not be given in a report if the report is accompanied by drawings, and probably should not be given even if the report must stand on its own. The fact that a girder in an area of interest is a 16-inch steel wide-flange is a necessary part of a report, the fact that it is a W16x31 is not. Unless the exact size of the beam is a point of interest, this is information best kept in the field notes.

The type of member information depends on the material. Wood structure is limited by the relative simplicity of possible connection types. Once the basic details of wood connection have been found (and documented either through photos or sketches), the only documentation of structure required is the listing of the type of wood (often given simply as the species) and the gross sizes of members. This information is usually written on architectural drawings in the same manner as the sizes and types of wood for finish use. The information is all relatively easy to obtain except for the species, which may never have been documented and can only be determined from samples by specialized labs.

Industrial materials have many more variables to be defined. Cast-iron columns, the first industrial building material in common use, require not only definition of the column size and wall thickness, but also details of the connections of the columns to one another at splices and to floor beams. Prefabricated members, such as iron (and later steel) beams require size definition, connection definition, and material property definition, all of them more complicated than the equivalent information for wood.

Industrial materials that are specially made for the project, even if components are mass-produced (such as tile-arch floors and concrete slabs) require a great deal of information for definition. In a concrete slab, the location, bent shape, and size of each reinforcing rod (out of hundreds in a typical floor slab) may be different. Extremely complicated structure became more common in the twentieth century, as architects and engineers both explored the extents of design possible in steel and concrete. Structural design drawings changed from simple lists of beam and column sizes associated with the architecture to complicated diagrams of layout and assembly; investigation drawings for modern buildings are correspondingly more complex.

Complete documentation is always a part of investigation. It is foolish to make the effort to determine unknown basic information about a building's structure and not carefully record everything learned. Not all information belongs on the construction drawings eventually produced: excess information can confuse the contractors and occasionally even leads to higher bids when the scope of work is overestimated. This does not mean that all information does not belong on an organized drawing. Field notebooks are often the personal property of the individual engineer or architect, and the information in them is rarely reproduced and properly filed. A good solution is to take a set of sepias or other reproducible copies of the drawings and add all of the information from the field notes, including the date of the investigation, creating a set of existing-condition drawings for the date.

Whether or not the information found in a specific source is pertinent, the sources should all be listed in the report, either in the introduction or in an appendix. This allows future investigators to use the report as a resource without reproducing all of the work that went into creating it.

Incorporating Field Data into Design Documents

If field investigation is the first step toward performing physical alteration or preservation work, the field information may be used for new design drawings and not for a report. In this case, the field information is often written down on an early generation of the design drawings—in other words, a rough picture of the building is created so that exact field information can be written down in the same place and on the same drawing where it will appear in final design.

Design drawings for renovation and alteration must distinguish between existing building elements and new. Various graphic notations have been used to distinguish new from old, including the use of different hatches (e.g., hatched for new and unhatched for old), line types (e.g., solid lines for new and dashed lines for old), and line weight (e.g., heavy lines for new and light or halftone lines for old). The development of computer drafting and color printing have made this easier, and it is now as simple to use a different color or line type to identify elements as it is to draw new elements. Visual identification of this type requires consistency across all drawings, including plans, elevations, and details, and a clear key explaining the notation used.

Image manipulation, beginning with the xerographic copying of ordinary and rectified photos onto mylar drawing sheets and extended through the use of digital image manipulation, has allowed the creation of mixed-media "drawings." The most useful type of drawing produced this way is one that mixes drafted plans and elevations with photographs and text so that details that may be difficult to draw clearly are properly located and marked with appropriate information. This method has become very popular in the restoration of ornate facades because it eliminates the need to draw each detail of stone or terra-cotta ornament but still shows all of the detail. There is no downside to using digital image manipulation in design and presentation documents, but this method must be used very carefully in reports. Written reports are often used in legal proceedings, including sales and suits, and a manipulated image can create the impression that the person who prepared the report was attempting to deliberately mislead. Any significant changes to pictures, such as changing contrast to highlight a water stain, should be noted in the text or in an appendix.

7
Field Work

Descriptions of data and inspection methods are meaningless if the process of investigation is not organized on site. Organization can be as large a factor in the success of an investigation as the knowledge of the investigator is—a well-planned investigation by a novice will turn up information that a cursory glance by an expert may miss.

The core of an investigation is the process of walking through a building to gather and record information. No single method is best because situations vary depending on the building itself and the reason the investigation is taking place. An examination of a 20,000-square-foot brick wall that is one face of a twenty-story building will be different than an examination of a 20,000-square-foot brick wall that is one face of a long two-story warehouse.

Field Investigation

The simplest field investigation of a building is a walk-through to review and document the structural system based on observations of the finished surfaces and any exposed structure. Depending upon the investigator's previous field experience, familiarity with different types of construction specific to different eras, and the amount of information about the building available from document search, this simple technique may provide

THIS FLOOR WILL
SAFELY SUSTAIN
A LOAD OF [120] LBS
PER SQUARE FOOT

7-1. Documentation required by local building departments, such as this sign, are good indications of original design parameters, but not infallible.

all the information required for design. Visual examination sometimes reveals all of the required information. (Figure 7-1) For instance, in many wood-frame buildings, the joist size and spacing are visible at unfinished portions of the attic and basement. The details of concrete and steel buildings, however, are less apparent. The investigation's thoroughness will reflect the overall condition of the building, the extent of the repair or renovation to be performed, the amount of information available from other sources, and the time and budget allocated to preliminary studies. The more atypical the conditions, the more time the investigation will require.

A straightforward case is a minor renovation to a modern building where the original drawings are available, such as the installation of tenant stairs into a steel-framed office tower. Because the floor slab and framing are known, and the existence of unknown exceptional conditions very unlikely, it is possible to design the entire renovation without seeing the site and arrange for a site investigation during the finish demolition to verify the assumed conditions.

An example of a more complex case is a major renovation in an old building with a mixed structural system in poor condition. In a building from the early 1900s that has masonry bearing walls, steel beams, tile-arch floors, cast-iron columns, and steel framing and concrete slabs from previous renovations, it may be necessary to start from scratch with architectural floor plans and locate each structural member individually to create a framing plan. If the condition of the members is suspect because of weathering damage or overstress, there is no substitute for actual observation of the condition of every single member. If damage is expected and provisions have been made for repairs, simply exposing and examining enough members to confirm the damage may be necessary. This situation illustrates why an investigation can be less thorough if it is known that repairs will be needed. There is no need to thoroughly document conditions that will be removed or repaired; documentation of fair conditions for which minor repair or no action at all is anticipated, however, must be more comprehensive.

Field investigation must be performed in a systematic manner to reduce the frequency and extent of errors. It is safe to assume that a large-scale investigation will contain some small errors, which are usually discovered when the investigation results are used to create design drawings or during construction. There are sources that provide a framework for technical investigations, such as the American Society of Civil Engineers's "Guidelines for Structural Assessment of Existing Buildings." All of these sources emphasize the importance of repetitive collection of data to lessen the possibility of drawing false conclusions from out-of-the-ordinary facts. By examining a reasonable number of conditions of a given type (e.g., looking at many floor joists for decay fungi), the typical cases can be distinguished from the exceptions. The number of conditions that are "reasonable" varies with the goal of the investigation. For example, if the intent is to prove that repairs are required, two instances of damage are probably enough to make the case. If the intent is to prove that more investigation is required to reduce the expected amount of repair, ten or fifteen cases of damage may need to be examined. If the intent is to prove that a single, visible occurrence of damage is a fluke and no other repairs are necessary, every portion of the structure must be examined, since it is not possible to prove a negative through the examination of isolated samples.

Structural investigation entails more than identifying the members in the area of interest. Any changes in load intensity or path caused by alterations must be investigated. This may mean investigating the columns or transfer girders several floors below the area where an interior alteration is planned. The more regular the building framing is, the more basic structure can be extrapolated across multiple floors or large areas. The most extreme example of this would be speculative office buildings or single-purpose factories. Both of these building types are characterized by repetitive framing similar across many floors and the majority of the plan area. The other end of the framing spectrum is occupied by large private houses, where each floor may have a different layout and each portion of the building may have unique conditions created by double-height rooms, balconies, porches, and varying roof profiles. Because of the likelihood of entirely different layouts on each floor, private houses are among the most difficult buildings to understand simply by looking at architectural floor plans. Inspection of the layout on site should include an examination of floor sag. The pattern of sag reveals where wood joists are loaded, allowing for easier identification of bearing stud walls than is possible from drawings.

Assumptions based on finished surfaces must be checked to eliminate possibilities that appear similar but are structurally dissimilar. For example, all wood stairs tend to sag with age, but structural failure of a header beam adjacent to a stair may cause a similar sag. A crucial aspect of this work is separating incidental or isolated failure from overall failure. This is most readily achieved by looking for patterns of damage as opposed to concentrating on the exact location of each crack. Patterns usually tell the most comprehensive story.

Ironically, one of the best sources of information is damage created by people. An empty building that has been vandalized often has more of its structure and mechanical systems exposed than an occupied building in good condition. Plumbers and other tradesmen often cut holes in ceilings and walls to perform their work, exposing structure that might otherwise be hidden. (Figure 7-2) As with any form of unplanned alteration, too much incidental cutting can be dangerous—plumbers and electricians often cut through structural elements with no regard for the stability of the element in question. It is not unusual during the investigation of a private house to find a number of floor joists that have been so severely cut that they are effectively useless.

Answers to questions and other generally useful information can be found in areas that are not visible to someone standing on the ground or on a floor. The simplest method of examining a high ceiling or the lower

7-2. The hung light fixture in the lower right portion of the picture is suspended from a hanger rod drilled through the bottom flange of a steel beam in the floor above. The installation of the modern fixture did not include repair of the plaster ceiling, which is the fire protection for the beam.

reaches of walls is to climb an ordinary ladder. If work of some type is in progress or a contractor is available to help with the investigation, more sophisticated methods may be used, including (in order of increasing cost and complexity in set-up) standing scaffolding, rolling scaffolding, motorized scissors and bucket lifts, the exterior use of swing-stages, and other hanging scaffolds. Each of these methods has its advantages and disadvantages. Any time work is performed off the ground, the investigator must be trained in proper safety procedures by someone familiar with the equipment at hand.

Measurements

As an investigation continues, dimensions being measured become steadily smaller in scale. In the early stages, the measurements include gross data such as overall plan dimensions and column locations, although these may be determined secondhand through measurements of finish enclosures. Then partition and beam locations are noted, followed by floor openings, wall openings, and details of partitions such as short return walls at doors. The amount of detail pursued is dependent on why the investigation is being conducted and who is responsible for it. If a building is empty and is being investigated for safety and the possibility of reuse, gross dimensions and structural member sizes may be the only measurements required. If a building is occupied and is being examined before architectural modifications, exact locations and details of finishes and mechanical systems will be needed for design.

Gross physical measurement is often accompanied by surveying. Formal surveying can only be conducted by a licensed surveyor and will include precise measurement of the location, size, elevation, and shape of a building with respect to known benchmarks. Depending on the level of surveying desired, the benchmarks can be simply the property lines as marked, local benchmarks, or U.S. Geological Survey benchmarks. Informal surveying might include plumb-bob measurements of wall out-of-plumb dimensions or tape measurements of the building exterior relative to assumed property lines such as fences.

Tools in Field Investigation

Depending on the reason for the investigation and the experience of the investigator, various small tools may be of use. A clear choice is a flashlight for inspection in attics or other poorly lit spaces. Flashlights can be used in two ways that are not quite so obvious: they can illuminate a dark area so that a camera can be focused for a flash picture, and the beam of light can be shot sideways over a theoretically flat surface to reveal irregularities through their shadows. This can show out-of-plane defects not easily detected by direct observation.

An awl or a pocketknife can be used to check the consistency of wood and masonry. A dull knife blade or a secondary blade (such as the screwdriver on many utility pocketknives) is more useful than the regular knife blade—the purpose is to see how far the knife can penetrate into the material, not to cut it. When general conditions such as excessive moisture or visible surface damage such as insect entry holes and fungal growths exist, testing with a knife can give a fast answer to the extent of the problem. If the fungus is simply growing on the outside of the wood, regular hand pressure will not cause the point of the tool to penetrate the surface any more than it would penetrate fresh wood. Most forms of decay, however, reduce the wood density to the point where the tool can easily be pushed in. If it is possible to force an awl or dull knife blade into the wood, the wood is probably partially rotten or eaten by insects. Scraping mortar with a screwdriver or dull blade is an easy test of the cohesion of both lime and portland cement. Of course, a pocketknife is also a good tool for prying loose small pieces of mortar to take away for lab testing. Using a knife is also the first step from simple visual examination to probing.

An ordinary 25-foot steel tape is adequate for almost all measurements. Since most plan dimensions are broken by columns, intersecting partitions, or other obstructions, long straight measurements are rarely required. A 100-foot tape can be used for the exceptions, but requires two people to be used properly. Vertical measurements can often be obtained with a flexible tape by doubling the tape back so it will reach vertically, but this method is difficult to use for heights greater than a few feet and requires time, luck, and better-than-average coordination to produce consistently good results.

A folding carpenters' rule is more primitive than a steel tape, but it has the advantage of being stiff. The various segments of a rule can be set at right angles, making possible the measurement of a horizontal distance located 5 or 6 feet above the inspector's head. This practice is common in finding beams or joist width not visible from the floor above. Using a rule instead of a tape for overhead measurements is also easier and faster. (Figure 7-3)

7-3. Close-up of a spall in the top surface of a garage floor, showing the loose material removed and piled up at the left, calipers used to measure the reinforcing size, and waterproof crayon used for marking.

The best tool for quick determination of verticality is a plumb bob. The bob is simply a weight that is hung at the end of a string suspended next to the structural element being checked. When bobs are first hung, they have a tendency to swing as pendulums, showing any accidental sideways force during set-up. By allowing the swinging to die out or by carefully hand-damping the swings, the investigator can eventually obtain a true vertical against which walls and columns can be compared.

The information that an investigator should be collecting was described in chapter 6. The actual recording of data is best done in a bound field notebook or on drawings specifically marked for field use. Loose sheets of paper may be convenient on site (or may not, as they usually require the use of a clipboard) but are easily lost and damaged. A good notebook has a hard cover and can be held flat with one hand; field notebooks designed for construction use have waterproof covers and pages.

Safety On-site

Construction sites are inherently dangerous places and are made safe only through constant attention to safety procedures. Occupied or empty buildings are obviously less dangerous than construction sites, but they are still potentially dangerous to an investigator, who is in an unfamiliar place and usually walking (and climbing) in places not ordinarily visited, such as crawl spaces or attics. (Figure 7-4) The basic safety procedures for a construction site are therefore necessary for any investigation.

Part of safety on site can best be described as site etiquette. An investigator looking at a building, especially if construction is going on, is basically a stranger intruding in someone else's space. Many practices, such as checking in, are safety measures as well as signs of respect for those controlling and occupying the buiding. Check-in at a large construction site may require identification cards and clearing entry with a security guard, while at a small renovation or pre-purchase investigation it can be as simple as saying hello to the site superintendent. Regardless of the procedure, someone should always know when an investigator enters a building and how long the site visit is expected to take.

Investigations often take place in buildings or portions of buildings that have been secured with padlocks or self-locking doors. There are a number of simple practices that prevent accidental imprisonment: relocking padlocks on their hasps with the hasp open to make it clear to passersby

7-4. The public has been kept away from any danger that might exist in this abandoned building through the use of the fence and blocked-off window and door openings. Recent repairs to the brick are visible, but no guarantee of safe conditions inside.

that the door is intentionally open, blocking open self-closing doors with concrete blocks or other items heavy enough to stop the closing mechanism, and locking deadbolts with the door open, so that if the door does start to close it is blocked by its own lock.

The Occupational Safety and Health Administration (OSHA) of the U. S. Department of Labor defines the safety procedures used on construction sites in the United States. Similar government bodies exist in other countries, all with the same goal of defining safe practice for construction workers. While building investigators are rarely construction laborers, the logic of OSHA procedures applies to anyone who sets foot on a construction site and anyone climbing, crawling, or otherwise maneuvering around a site. Proper safety equipment will be marked as OSHA-approved, and general descriptions of approved precautions are available from local OSHA offices.

Beyond the OSHA regulations, common sense works as an appropriate guide. Before walking on a loose piece of plywood, note how it is supported—it may be covering a hole in the floor and it may not support a person's weight. Pay attention to where your hands, feet, and head are at all times—if those five parts of your body are safe, your torso almost certainly is as well. Never stick your head or hand into an open shaft (such as an elevator shaft), because you don't know when something will be coming up or down.

Dangerous materials are often found on construction sites, in abandoned buildings, and in obsolete construction assemblies that have been in continuous use for long periods of time. The most well known are asbestos and lead, which were widely used in construction for most of the twentieth century. Abandoned attics and protected portions of facades and roof may serve as nesting grounds for birds, bats, or other small animals. Fungus spores are another health threat that can be found in many buildings, particularly those that have recurrent roof or plumbing leaks or sealed ventilation systems. The best protection against inhaling or coming into contact with dangerous substances is to pay attention to their presence. Dust should not be assumed to be harmless unless its origin is known; contact with unknown materials should be avoided as much as possible.

Investigation Field Examples

The following examples are taken from actual buildings and represent the information gathered, in sequence, and some of the logical inferences drawn from that information. They are all composite examples, made from pieces of real-life investigations. What is observed, and therefore can be taken as fact, is kept distinct from what is inferred, and therefore may be wrong.

The examples have been selected to show a variety of building and damage types. In addition to these specific examples, the list of building types commonly seen includes:

- multistory loft buildings
- rowhouses
- freestanding private houses
- churches and other religious buildings
- schools

7-5. The decorative carving near the entrance door gives the best evidence of the construction date an investigator is likely to find.

- theaters
- high-rise office buildings
- factories
- apartment houses
- barns
- single-level malls

Walk-through of a school

The building is a large, partially empty elementary school in an inner-city neighborhood. The neighborhood is generally known to have experienced its greatest growth in the late nineteenth century; the decorative carved date at the main entrance strongly suggests 1897 as the construction date. (Figure 7-5) The architectural style of the building—a simplified collegiate gothic—is appropriate for that era.

The base of the street facades is carved stone, the field of masonry above is brick, and the trim masonry on the upper stories is terra cotta. The terra cotta can be distinguished from stone or pre-cast concrete by fine cracks in the glaze covering. There is extensive damage to the facades, some properly repaired, some badly repaired, and some not

7-6. Original masonry can be distinguished from repairs by gaps in the trim pattern, the sloppiness of the more recent work compared with the original construction, and the relative lack of dirt on the new brick.

repaired. Figure 7-6 shows relatively new brick replacing original brick and terra-cotta trim on a street facade. Not only does the brick not match, disturbing the building's appearance, but the stains and bulging of the repairs suggest that the symptoms (eroding mortar and shifting or cracking brick) were remedied without addressing the cause (water entry into the walls). The heavy staining below every window strongly suggests the window sills as a primary source of water.

Figure 7-7 shows the typical conditions at the rear facades. The walls are built solidly of common brick, with steel channel lintels over the windows. The paint coating on the brick has worn off in areas that receive more than average amounts of water—such as the sides of the window openings, where water from the lintel drips down. There have been brick repairs at the roof leader on the second pier from the right, indicating that the leader leaked heavily before the visible repairs.

More extensive damage is visible in some parts of the courtyard. (Figure 7-8) The open joints in the low wall seen to the left of the parked car indicate little or no maintenance as well as the effect of rainwater seeping through the slate capstone joints. The building superintendent men-

7-7. This rear facade shows the neglect typical of the less visible portions of many buildings. Much of the building's construction is visible, as well as weathering of both masonry and steel.

7-8. This courtyard is obviously used by people parking their cars, but the extreme damage to both masonry and windows has not been repaired.

7-9. A cast-iron column base in a cellar. This cellar was the only place in the building where the columns were directly visible.

tioned that the courtyard is occasionally used to store trucks; the impact damage to the wall corner is the result of a lack of bollards or other protective devices in an area not originally meant for vehicular use. Finally, the pattern of missing paint and extensive brick damage on the pier separating the narrow window from the adjacent wide window shows particularly poor drainage in this area.

The interior of the school retains most of its original finishes, including circular plaster enclosures around each column. The column spacing, visible despite the finishes, was measured as typically 18 feet center to center, with some irregularities around stairs. No indication of the structure of the building can be obtained within the finished spaces of classrooms and hallways. In the basement, used only for storage and mechanical systems, the structure is partly exposed. Figure 7-9 shows the base of a column in a storage room. While the visible metal could be any form of iron, the form of the base "plate"—two plates connected with a series of vertical stiffeners—and the connection between the column and base plate—simple machine bolts—both indicate cast iron. Figure 7-10 shows the top of the same column. The visible portion of the beam-to-column connections—the vertical stiffeners of seated connections—are consistent with

7-10. The top of a cast iron column, showing the bottom of the beam support brackets.

cast-iron construction. In addition, the double stiffeners on two sides of the column are consistent with iron and steel beam design practice before 1920. The double stiffeners are present when double beams are used as girders.

Figure 7-10 also shows that there have been changes in the building's plumbing. The galvanized iron pipe running vertically at the right side of the picture and horizontally at the top of the picture is relatively new drain pipe. The small copper pipe running horizontally on the right side of the picture is new water supply pipe. An architectural survey of the first floor found the expanded restrooms served by these pipes.

From the information already known, certain assumptions can be made about the basic structure of the building. By 1897, steel had replaced wrought iron in building use. The presence of cast-iron columns and the extreme thickness of the exterior walls (measured as up to 24 inches for a building with four full floors and a partial penthouse) suggest that the exterior walls are partly bearing, carrying lateral loads and some of the interior floor loads. The floor beams are small steel I-beams, with doubled I-beams as girders.

In one basement hallway, the plaster ceiling had collapsed or been

7-11. Failure of the plaster ceiling has exposed the underside of the tile-arch floor above.

removed, exposing the floor structure above. (Figure 7-11) The floor is seen to be terra-cotta tile flat arches, which again is consistent with the known structural facts. The orientation of the arches can be determined from the shape of the tiles: the narrow strip of tile to the right of the left light support is the center of the arch (the "keystone"), while the more-or-less unmortared joint to the right of the right light support is the juncture of two arches at a floor beam. The next beam location is halfway between the left light support and the left edge of the plaster. Tile arches are quite fragile, and the installation of the modern fluorescent lights is seen to have caused damage at the left light support, where a section of the tile is missing.

This type of structure was generally designed for higher loads than required by modern codes, and is adequate for any ordinary use as long as weathering damage can be controlled. The initial walk-through indicates that the exterior conditions need closer examination and moderately extensive repair of the masonry.

Walk-through of a loft building

The age of the building is unknown. However, the area is known to have been built up in the 1920s. As far as the rental records show, the building

7-12. Not much information can be gained by studying this loft-building facade. Recent alterations and original material are both coated, providing a uniform, although not pristine, appearance.

7-13. The stucco coating obscures the base material of the wall, but the cracking and filled-in windows are visible.

has been continuously occupied by light manufacturing and warehousing businesses. There are no original construction drawings available.

From across the street, the main portion of the building is seen to be five stories high with no setbacks in front and a tan stucco facade. The alleys on both sides and the narrow yard in the rear allow direct observation of all facades, which shows that there are no setbacks on any side. The relatively short street and rear facades (approximately 80 feet long) have wide windows that fill the bays between the piers that are assumed to mark column bays. (Figure 7-12) The 150-foot-long side facades have much smaller "punched" window openings. (Figure 7-13)

Two forms of exterior damage are endemic: cracks on the side facades (as seen in Figure 7-13) that typically start and end at windows, and random cracking in the street and rear facades, as seen in Figure 7-14). The nature of these cracks cannot be determined until the structural system of the building is known, but random cracks are rarely structural. The cracks running from window to window could be serious if the side walls are bearing walls.

7-14. The sliding aluminum windows are a relatively modern element, and not original to a building known to date from before 1940.

Because the building is used for industry, its interior is easily accessible to investigation. Another form of damage is common on the interior—floor top-surface cracks, visible in Figure 7-15. All of these cracks have worn edges, indicating that they are not recent. As with the side-wall cracks, the severity of damage indicated by these cracks cannot be determined until the structural system is known.

The first indication of the structural system is a column in a storage room off the main entrance lobby. This column (Figure 7-16) at first glance appears to be approximately 5 feet square in section and have a serious crack at one corner. In reality, sounding the "column" surfaces shows it to be a hollow enclosure, meaning that the crack is structurally meaningless. Two visual clues provide the answer to the building's construction. First, the concrete ceiling steps down around the column enclosure—the small vertical surface between the main ceiling and the lowered area at the column is visible next to the photograph's date stamp. Second, the small bulge on the left side of the column where it meets the lowered ceiling makes sense in only one way, as the flared capital of a round column. If a building this age has a concrete frame with columns and flared capitals, it would be expected to have drop panels, which would explain the lowered ceiling.

Further exploration discovers columns without enclosures (such as that visible in Figure 7-17), confirming a concrete frame with two-way slab floors as the basic structural type. This implies that the exterior walls are stuccoed masonry that is supported on the frame, and not load bearing. While this conclusion does not mean that the exterior damage is not potentially dangerous (since falling masonry is dangerous regardless of its original function), it does eliminate the cracking as a sign of potential structural failure.

The floor cracking noted earlier is common in heavily loaded two-way slabs. Reinforced concrete cracks as loads are redistributed within, and any mismatch in geometry between the loading patterns and the reinforcing layout results in cracks that seem to be randomly located.

7-15. Cracks in a concrete floor slab.

7-16. The underside of the floor above shows the board marks and nail holes of old concrete, while the column sides are, where uncracked, entirely smooth.

7-17. A typical concrete column with a mushroom capital and drop panel from the 1910s to the 1930s.

The interior partitions are concrete block, as seen in Figure 7-17. Because the block and the concrete will move differently when subjected to load, it can be expected that there will be cracks where block abuts concrete.

A last form of damage found in the interior confirms the construction and provides a source of concern. The inside face of several columns and beams located at the exterior walls are badly damaged. The reinforcing in the column in Figure 7-18 is still solid to the touch, but must be considered potentially dangerous, since reinforced concrete columns depend for strength on the rebar being confined by concrete. The reinforcing at the beam in Figure 7-19 has lost significant amounts of steel, and therefore is known to have lost load-bearing capacity. These conditions are the most serious observed in the building, and require structural analysis of the actual loads and capacities before the building can be assumed to be safe.

7-18. A small spall on a concrete column. Not dangerous in itself, but possibly a sign of destructive mechanisms (e.g., rusting of the rebar) at work. Note the crack directly above the spall: this is an earlier stage of the same type of failure.

7-19. Severe spalling of concrete on the bottom of a beam. Not only does this remove the fire- and waterproofing for the rebar, but it reduces the load capacity of the beam.

Walk-through of an apartment house

This investigation was conducted immediately after a fire that caused severe damage to the building. Only the basic examination is described here, as discovering the causes of fire are beyond the scope of ordinary investigation and the skills of most investigators.

The apartment house is a local landmark and is known to have been built in 1904 to the design of a prominent architectural firm. A partial set of original architectural drawings is available, but no structural drawings.

The building's plan is a rough "H" shape, with flat side street facades and courtyards facing the main street in front and the rear yard. The building is eleven stories tall with no setbacks. The only major variation in the exterior above the first floor is the presence of a two-story mansard roof covered with slate. (Figure 7-20)

Exterior restoration work was in progress at the time of the fire. The work included cleaning and repairing the brick and terra-cotta facades as well as the slate roofs. The south wing of the building is covered by access scaffolding (Figure 7-21), which was damaged in the fire along with the building itself.

7-20. Facades built of the ornamental materials of the beginning of the twentieth century: pressed brick, terra cotta, and slate.

7-21. Standing scaffolding used for facade renovation on an apartment house. Note the netting to prevent dropped objects from reaching occupied sidewalks below.

Given the age of the building, and the fact that it was built as an apartment house rather than for commercial use, its structural type cannot be assumed. The building was constructed at a time when bearing-wall systems and mixed systems of partial iron framing and bearing walls were still in use for tall apartment houses, even though steel frames dominated commercial high-rise construction. The presence of large storefront windows at the ground floor does not provide useful information, since records indicate that the installation of the storefronts took place between twenty and forty years after the original construction.

A fast walk-through of several apartments provides no useful information, since all of the structure is covered by plaster ceilings and partitions. The fire-damaged area is useful for this investigation, as the structure was exposed by damage to the finishes. Figure 7-22 is typical of the damaged area, with a portion of the mansard facing the front courtyard on the left and damaged scaffolding on the right. The planes of the roof, without the

7-22. Fire damage has revealed the terra-cotta tile of the mansard roof at left, the metal flashing at the lower left once hidden by shingles, and the steel framing around the windows. The damaged scaffolding at right was unsafe for use in examining the building proper.

7-23. The steel frame in the center, warped by the heat of the fire, provides the basic support for a window. The burned wood on the right is an actual window frame.

slate, are seen to be terra-cotta tile. The bay window at the center of the picture is supported on steel outrigger beams; the roof level beams are visible through the open window as dark stripes against the lighter background of terra-cotta tile floor. Further investigation on the interior reveals steel columns (for example, the dark vertical stripe behind the bent window frame in Figure 7-23), confirming that the building was designed with a full steel frame and that damage to the walls does not threaten structural stability. This information is sufficient to allow the fire investigation to proceed without evacuating the undamaged portions of the building.

8
Probing

As field investigation gets more detailed and more intense, hidden portions of the structure become a steadily greater impediment to finding useful facts. For a basic investigation, looking at finished surfaces provides enough information to proceed with design or write a simple report. For a thorough condition report or extensive alteration design, measurement of hidden structure may be necessary. "Probing" is the act of removing unimportant or replaceable material to allow investigation of the more important, hidden structure. In the most extreme cases, probing may be used to reveal and document the entire building structure for analysis. Because it causes extensive disruption, this type of probing cannot ordinarily be used to determine the feasibility of alteration or expansion, but is ordinarily part of the design phase.

The decision to probe is based on a number of factors, some of which may not be under the control of the investigator. Probing is rarely allowed during prepurchase investigation, (when the investigator's client does not own the building) even if the probes are to be repaired after examination. Occupied spaces are rarely available for probing because of the noise and dirt created by the process of physically cutting apart portions of the finishes; when probes can be made in such spaces, they usually require more than a nominal repair. If the space has highly ornamental or historic finishes, the problems are greatly multiplied. Probing under these conditions should be considered a last resort.

Probing includes a wide range of activities, all of which expose structural members for observation of their condition. The success of probing activities depends on the designer's experience in reviewing the conditions and in locating the probes so that they fairly represent the structure. Probing is the simplest form of destructive testing and provides only visual information. The least destructive probe is the removal of finished surfaces in a small area to expose one condition—for example, cutting a hole in a dropped gypsum-board ceiling to expose a beam-to-column connection not entirely detailed on existing drawings. Probing can be extended to a series of small openings—to measure several column sizes, for example—and finally to large areas, such as pulling down an entire ceiling to expose the condition of wood floor joists above. (Figures 8-1, 8-2, 8-3)

Probing through finishes is as safe as any construction operation can be, as long as ordinary safety precautions are observed for such dangers

8-1. The irregular brick revealed by the removal of the plaster finish in a nineteenth-century rowhouse is typical of unfinished masonry work. The horizontal stripes (at roughly the mid-height of the abandoned door frame and just above the door frame) are wood nailers set into the brick to allow easy attachment for the original wood strip lath.

8-2. This garage has wood columns supporting wrought-iron or steel girders. The remainder of the floor structure is hidden by a sheet tin ceiling. Removal of a section of ceiling shows wood joists, suggesting that the building may have been originally built as a stable. Note the cast-iron cap plate on the column supporting the beam ends.

8-3. Removal of a mismatched section of ceiling in the garage reveals that the section of floor directly above is a modern alteration with steel deck.

as live electrical lines hidden within walls. Often, simply exposing the surface of the hidden structure provides inadequate structural information, although it may provide some basic data as concrete column sizes or filler beam spacing. The next step is the removal of materials that are lightly stressed, but part of the basic building structure, such as masonry fireproofing around a steel column, concrete encasement on a steel beam, bottom rebar cover in a concrete slab, or a few bricks in a bearing wall. (Figures 8-4, 8-5) This type of probe is useful for obtaining access to the critical portions of structural members for measurement.

The line between easily removable structure and vital structure is not always clear, even during the probing process. Unusual rebar configurations in flat-slab buildings with irregular layouts can result in bars ending in unexpected locations. If the bottom cover is removed to expose the bars to allow for the slab capacity to be determined, the bar's tensile capacity may be accidentally reduced. A floor slab protected by cement finish on top and a plaster ceiling below may turn out to be a flat tile arch rather than the expected concrete, and the probe that exposes this fact can destroy the arch bearing at one end. Even the safest probe can lead to disastrous collapse if the original structure was built incorrectly. Thus,

8-4. An extensive probe of the spandrel beam and hung lintel below an area of damaged brick. Note the shoring: by propping the brick at several locations, the entire wall is supported.

8-5. A close-up of a damaged steel hung lintel and support brackets exposed by a probe.

a preliminary determination of the type of structure to be removed should be made before probing begins. One example of the potential for collapse (which was quite serious because of the building type and proposed loading) took place in a multistory industrial building. The rivets in the beam and girder connections in the concrete-encased steel frame were missing at a number of locations. The loose beams were resting on the two inches of concrete column encasement, which was being removed to expose the connections for examination.

The possible dangers of damage caused by examination necessitate the engineer's presence during probing. The probes must be carried out in a careful and deliberate manner, and the condition of the structure should be checked at all times to ensure that the examination does not lead to any failure. An improperly placed probe can destroy a steel connection or the continuity of a concrete joint. The logic of locating probes is exactly the same as the logic of designing a new structure; the critical locations are the same and familiar to any designer. Typically, probes for material information are taken at areas of low stress, while probes for damage may have to be taken at areas of high stress.

The most potentially informative probe commonly performed is the removal of small pieces of the actual structure for observation and testing. This form of probing, often called "coupon testing" after the size and shape of the pieces of steel used, is necessary when the actual materials used must be defined but may interfere with stability because of the removal of actual structure. A small piece of a wood joist can be removed to determine the wood species and moisture content and therefore its allowable flexural and shear stresses. A small piece of old steel or wrought iron can be tested for chemical composition, including impurities such as sulfur or silicon that would interfere with welding, and for mechanical properties such as yield and ultimate stress. Cores can be drilled from existing concrete and tested for their ultimate compressive stress in much the same manner as the testing of cylinders created during a concrete pour. (Figures 8-6, 8-7) Chemical tests can also be performed for chloride ion content and electrolytic potential. These tests provide allowable stresses that can be used in the process of alteration design.

Professionals investigating a building have little to do with the tests beyond ordering them, and locating which material can be removed without interfering with the stability and safety of the building. The difficulty

8-6. Using a core drill to take samples from a concrete slab floor. Note that the raised computer floor has been removed to expose the concrete top surface.

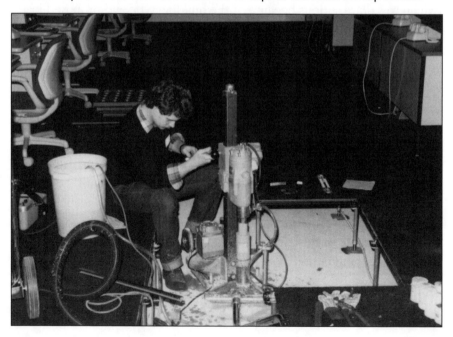

8-7. Concrete cores taken from a slab for lab testing.

is in finding accessible locations of low stress where the removal of material is possible. The most common location of coupon removal from steel beams is the lower flange at a simple connection; for concrete floor slabs, cores are usually taken near a span end. Removal of samples from all members is not possible. Heavily loaded columns should not be interfered with when samples can be taken from filler beams of the same age. Similarly, samples should come from filler beams, not girders, from the middle-middle strip of flat plate floors, and from joists and not their supporting beams.

Depending on the type of probing being performed, the level of knowledge about the building, and the contractual relationships involved, the designers may or may not be present during the probing process. On large projects, the contractor cutting the probes may be required to obtain a consulting engineer to examine stability during probing. The more available information about the existing structure and the less important the material to be removed is, the less supervision is required. For example, the removal of acoustical tile ceilings in a fairly new office building where drawings are available requires little or no supervision.

There are exceptions that can confuse the issue of finding representative samples. If the material in the building is not relatively homogeneous, or if alterations were made at some time before the investigation, structural elements that appear similar may have significantly different physical properties. A common location for this type of peculiarity is within the metal frames of buildings built between 1885 and 1900. Steel was replacing wrought iron in construction during this period, but the quality of steel produced by different mills was variable, and the economics of using the two metals varied greatly with the locale and the year. As a result, it is possible to find buildings of mixed wrought iron and steel, and there is no easy method to distinguish between the two metals. In one extreme case, box columns built up of a pair of channels and a pair of cover plates were themselves not homogeneous: the channels were good-quality rolled steel, while the plates were wrought iron with higher-than-desirable levels of silicon and sulfur. A more common and easier-to-discover example is the presence of replacement joists in a wood-floor building. The newer joists may be of a different species or grade of wood than the original material, and therefore may have lower allowable stresses. Depending on the age of the original joists and the newer joists, their dimensions may not be the same. Lumber has been cut to the same nominal dimensions since the 1830s (e.g., a 2x4 is nominally 2 inches by 4 inches), but the actual size has varied. When cut lumber first became commercially available, the actual sizes matched the nominal sizes. Because lumber is planed after being cut, the actual sizes gradually became smaller, so that a 2x4 is 1½ inches thick and 3½ inches wide. If a building is old enough, it may contain lumber that is larger than the modern final size; since the size affects strength, the old portions may be stronger than expected. The following example shows another type of difference within a structure. An investigation of weathering damage to a high-rise, concrete-frame apartment house showed that the vast majority of the damage was caused by the rebar in the projecting slab edges being too close to the surface, but one balcony had anomalous cracking. As a small portion of concrete was being removed to examine the rebar, it became clear that the balcony concrete was very weak and full of voids. While there is no obvious clue as to why this one portion of concrete, some 4 feet wide and 10 feet long, should be in poor condition, it was probably from a different truck than those on adjacent floors, and placed in inclement weather.

Probing that includes removal of samples can be considered the least disruptive form of destructive testing. The damage caused by most probes can be easily repaired (or at least the finishes can be patched to prevent danger to the building occupants) while full-scale destructive testing may leave nothing of the tested area worth saving. Often, the probe patches can be done cheaply, in all senses of the word, since the area in question will be thoroughly ravaged by construction shortly afterward. Even when temporary architectural repairs are required, as in interior renovations of occupied space, the repairs need not comply with ordinary standards of care so long as they are not actively unsafe.

The final common type of probing can best be described as selective demolition probing. Material that has been scheduled for demolition is removed in the presence of the engineer responsible for the design of new structure. The engineer can use the opportunity to investigate the existing conditions and call for shoring and stabilization of the existing structure as required. This is a critical tool in cases where information about the building is insufficient to allow for detailed demolition instructions to be produced. Unfortunately, it is also inherently dangerous because actual structure is being disrupted while the building is not considered a construction site and may be occupied.

Progress in selective demolition is extremely slow when the work must be halted regularly to allow for engineer's inspections and the insertion of shoring. The extra cost associated with the delay is justified when the extent of damage or the capacity of framing are unknown. Ordinary investigation, including probing, can usually determine enough information to obviate the need for this technique, leaving its use for the less typical parts of buildings. Areas where the manner of construction is not readily visible and may differ substantially from the surroundings include mechanical and elevator shafts, stairwells, alterations such as the filling in of an internal court, rooftop additions, and filled-in openings of any type in floors, walls, or roofs. In these settings, frame buildings may contain bearing walls; bearing-wall buildings, posts; concrete buildings, steel beams; fireproof buildings, wood-joist floors. Older buildings may contain types of structure considered archaic, such as steel angle frames infilled with terra cotta surrounding elevator shafts. Once the construction type is identified, the expected details can be identified, although nothing can be counted on until seen.

The logic of selective demolition probing is the same as any other probing or demolition work. The goal is to avoid undermining any remaining structure as each piece of the building is removed, even if those pieces are as small as individual bricks. When, for example, a steel beam is found supporting a brick wall, it is not always clear if the beam is wall bearing or frames into a post. The portion of the wall that could possibly be supporting the beam must remain undisturbed until the end condition is determined. This type of uncertainty is overcome piecemeal by removing material known to be unloaded and reobserving the structure.

Location

Probe location is affected not only by stress and load-disruption concerns but also by the more mundane concerns of accessibility and economics. If the logical location for a probe is in a difficult-to-reach place, such as on the facade's exterior or the ceiling over a large, open space (like a theater or gym), providing access may be prohibitively expensive. Hung scaffolding, such as is needed for exterior access, is expensive and disruptive; the methods used to provide high interior access, such as mechanical lifts and staging, vary widely in price but are all very disruptive to the spaces.

One of the many judgment calls that must be made in deciding how and where to probe structure is when to use money that would be spent on providing accessibility to provide instead extra probes in easier-to-reach locations. Another trade-off is creating more numerous probes through finishes as opposed to fewer structural probes. Since the idea of probing is to perform fast and inexpensive work that provides information that would otherwise not be known until construction, placing probes in locations where expensive scaffolding is required is self-defeating. Given the choice between an easily accessible probe location and a remote one, the accessible location should be chosen unless there is a reason to believe that the remote location has information that cannot be found elsewhere.

Special Documentation

Professionals produce various forms of documentation in the course of directing probes. The most useful and common is a set of plans showing the location of each probe. A note can be appended to the plan at each probe location calling out the size and type of probe required (e.g., "Remove face brick in a 2' by 2' square, centered on paint mark, to expose back-up brick") or the probes can be numbered and a key provided. (Figures 8-8, 8-9) The more probes created and the more repetitive they are, the more useful the number-and-key system becomes. The probe plans can be used to write field notes on the conditions observed, creating a compact record of this phase of investigation.

Probe details are used to supplement probe plans when the demolition is in complicated patterns or the structure exposed after the initial removal of the surface requires special treatment. The details are similar to the details used in construction or selective demolition during construction, and they are usually keyed to the probing plans.

MEMORANDUM

To:

From: Date: 12-21-99   Project No.:

Project: # of Pages: 3

Subject: Probe Locations

Please provide probes at the upper and lower balconies as indicated on the attached sketch. These probes are required to verify the existing structural framing detailing.

The following is a description of the six probes required:
1. Remove wall finish and masonry to expose steel connection where lower balcony girder connects to north wall column.
2. Remove wall finish and masonry to expose steel connection where upper balcony girder connects to north wall beam.
3. Remove wall finish and masonry up to 2 feet above finish floor and 2 feet below finish ceiling of lower balcony.
4. Remove wall finish and masonry up to 2 feet above finish floor and 2 feet below finish ceiling of upper balcony.
5. Remove floor finish and ceiling finish on lower balcony around column 18 per dimensions shown.
6. Remove floor finish and ceiling finish on upper balcony around column 18 per dimensions shown.

Please contact me if you have any questions or need clarification.

8-8. Notes providing details of probes to be opened.

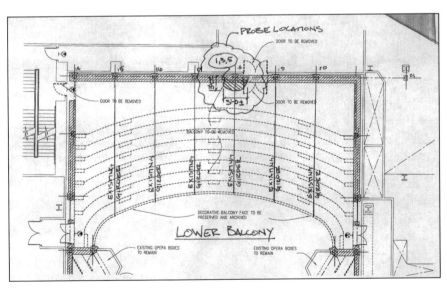

8-9. A plan showing locations of probes 1, 3, and 5.

Probing

151

In cases where making probes through heavily ornamented finished surfaces is unavoidable, the best probe locator is a marked photograph similar to those described in chapter 6. This allows for exact delineation of areas to be removed and areas to remain and provides a record of the finishes being removed, which will be useful when the probe needs to be repaired.

Repairs

In most cases, probes must be repaired after the investigation is complete. If the probes are in an occupied portion of a building, repairs may be extensive, including plaster and paint work to restore the damaged finishes to their original appearance. This phrase "restore to original appearance" is often used in the probing specification to indicate to the probing contractor that simply providing a coat of paint is not sufficient; the area damaged by the probes must be fully restored.

If the probes are in an unoccupied area of a building or an area due to receive more intensive work during construction, restoration may be limited to repairing any damaged water- or fireproofing and providing a basic cover (often plywood) to close off the holes created.

Repairs are rarely addressed in probe documents for two reasons. First, probes are usually part of an investigation that leads to more work, so extensive repairs may not be necessary. Second, probes are often performed under some type of time pressure, whether it is caused by a tight schedule for investigation and design or by restrictions on when the noisy and messy work of probing is allowed. In either case, careful repair of finishes is often delayed until the investigation is complete—that is, when construction begins in a design-oriented investigation, and when the report has been finalized for a condition assessment or feasibility investigation.

9
Testing

The word "testing" can cover a great many activities when applied to construction. Analysis on paper of structural adequacy and probing have been called testing by various authorities. In the context of this book, testing refers to the physical testing of materials or assemblies adequate according to a known standard. Materials tests on hidden material either accompany probes or take place during the early stages of construction. Sometimes exposed materials, such as facade elements, can be tested in situ, but more often the piece to be tested is removed and sent to a lab. Because lab tests take place under controlled conditions with equipment readily available, they tend to be more accurate and complete than field tests.

The phrase "lab tests" refers to a form of destructive test that can be performed in the lab or on site. The physical examination of building material under laboratory conditions requires removing pieces from the uncontrolled environment of the building in question. This removal makes the tested material unusable for building use. Nondestructive tests are performed on site and on material that is in its permanent location.

Destructive tests that are of interest include:

- probing, as described in the previous chapter
- destructive testing of samples
- load testing
- flood testing

Nondestructive tests that can be performed during an investigation include:

- flat-jack stress tests
- sounding
- sonic, thermal, magnetic resonance, or x-ray imaging
- test pits and borings
- crack monitoring
- vibration monitoring
- thermal and moisture monitoring

Examination methods other than testing (document searches, visual observation, probing) do not require specialty contractors. Demolition for probes is often conducted either by handymen (in the case of simple finish removal) or by the same contractor who will perform the planned alterations or preservation work. All of the forms of testing described here, on the other hand, require technicians with special training, specialized equipment, laboratories, or some combination of the three.

Certain situations call for testing. Material-sample testing is the most common and is closely related to the materials tests that take place during construction. If the strength of a material (for example, the mortar in a masonry wall) is critical to the evaluation being performed, a test of the mortar is usually performed even if documentation is available. Full-scale load testing is the most rare because of the extent of the work required to create an accurate load, monitor the test, analyze the results, and provide adequate safety provisions against structural failure during the test.

Destructive Testing

Two types of structural testing are properly described as destructive testing. The first is testing to failure, which finds the ultimate strength of the material or assembly tested and allows for extensive structural analysis, such as would be performed for a large alteration. The second is testing to a specified stress or load level, without regard for destructive consequences, and is often performed during a safety analysis. The first type, even if performed in situ, allows for preparation for failure and replacement. The second is often more ambiguous.

The coupon and core testing described as part of probing are types of small-scale destructive testing. The cores removed from existing concrete are usually crushed to determine the concrete's ultimate strength. Other tests performed on concrete samples include porosity testing and chemical analysis for destructive constituents such as chloride ions. In both cases, there is nothing left of the core after the tests are complete. The steel coupons can be tested to failure to determine the ultimate yield strength of the material, sliced apart for microstructure examination, or chemically tested for the percentage of carbon and trace elements. The structure as a whole is not affected, and since the portions of material removed are selected for their lack of importance, this type of testing is considered a probe.

Destructive testing of entire steel or concrete elements is rare. These materials are "designed," so if their design parameters (the allowable stresses) are known, the design calculations can be recreated. Sample testing is used to find the allowable stresses, and geometric examination and surface probing will determine the member configuration.

Destructive testing of wood structures is difficult if there are no members that can be entirely sacrificed. Unlike steel or concrete construction, a wood floor may not contain any areas that are understressed enough to permit their removal. This anomaly is due to wood's status as the only nonisotropic (material properties varying with direction) structural material. A typical wood beam has to be designed not only for the bending stress in the outermost flexural fibers, but also for horizontal shear stress at the supports, because the allowable stress value parallel to the grain is so much lower than the value perpendicular to the grain. By orienting wood beams with the grain parallel to the beam axis, we strengthen them in bending but weaken them at their point of highest relative shear stress. A coupon cannot be safely taken from the end as it can with a steel beam. The only location on a wood joist that may be safe for coupon removal is the compression side, midway between the location of the highest shear and highest flexural stresses. This location, which would be considered dangerous for probing in a steel frame, is acceptable due to the cooperative nature of wood construction, with load sharing taking place between the joists and subfloor. While the wood code allows for notching and round holes in beams, it sets very specific requirements as to size and placement. These requirements must be followed as closely during investigation as in new construction. Often, a small piece of joist will be found loose from the natural checking of the wood. Since a 3-by-1-inch piece is generally sufficient, these naturally occurring fragments can be used as coupons. Actual stress testing generally requires a full joist.

The best solution to the dilemma of finding adequate pieces of wood to test is to sacrifice an entire member. If the planned alterations entail removing joists or pieces of joists (for example, the cutting of stair opening that requires the shortening of a half-dozen joists) those pieces are adequate for testing. Their removal will be performed out of sequence— that is, long before they would be removed in the normal course of construction—if information is to be available for design. Due to the variable nature of the material, actual testing of a piece's capability of withstanding bending or shear stress requires several large samples. A better solution is to send pieces to a lab that specializes in wood analysis, which can identify the wood species and thus indirectly provide the design information required.

Beyond the destructive testing of materials and individual members, there are in-use tests that may not seem destructive but often are. Full-scale load testing, where ultimate load capacity is tested by loading a portion of an existing structure beyond its ordinary working loads, does not obviously damage a structure but can result in a complete collapse and therefore must be considered destructive. Load testing can include floor systems and complete frame assemblies. The floor area is loaded far beyond the loads expected in normal service. For example, the modern building codes allow for testing of preexisting assemblies provided that the loads used in testing are a stated percentage greater than the true dead load and 170% of the code-mandated live load. This means that the floor will be exposed to stress levels that theoretically reduce the safety factor to 1 or slightly less. Such extreme conditions are necessary to justify the acceptance of unknown conditions but can easily lead to failures of structures not capable of withstanding such overloads. When arranging such tests, prior analysis of the effect of collapse on adjacent structure must be performed: if the failure of the tested element or assembly can cause failure of another structure (for example, a floor slab falling onto and overloading a floor slab below), then the other structure must be protected or shored to prevent its failure or the test must be redesigned.

In a controlled-load, full-scale test, the structure must be examined afterward to determine whether any damage that calls into question the soundness of the structure has taken place. This is done both to see if damage has occurred that would make the test a failure and, even if the test is considered successful, for the future use of the tested structure after its intentional overload. The tested material is often monitored with strain gauges to develop a detailed picture of the structure's performance.

Another potentially destructive nondestructive test is the flood testing of roofs. This is a nonstructural test to determine if waterproofing works or, more often, to find an existing leak. An area is temporarily dammed off, or a drain temporarily stopped, so that a portion of a roof can be put under water in a controlled manner. Beyond being possibly damaged by water from the test, it is possible for a roof with unseen structural damage to collapse under the weight of the water.

Nondestructive Testing

While nondestructive testing might seem to logically follow field investigation as a nonintrusive research technique, its expense and frequent lack of complete results make it the least common research method. Testing without endangering the tested material requires high-technology testing techniques both to find the desired data and to ensure that the material remaining in service is undamaged. The most easily found benchmark in any sort of testing is complete failure of the test sample. That is why the earliest organized research into material properties in the mid-nineteenth century was based on the ultimate strength of the material. Even when people recognized that a beam or column becomes useless long before ultimate failure, they had no means to test actual stresses. As research into the physical properties of structural materials continued through the end of the nineteenth century and into the twentieth, more sophisticated lab tests were performed to determine the action of materials under differing degrees of stress. The basic idea behind nondestructive testing is to find, if only indirectly, actual and allowable stresses and material defects without causing failure.

No nondestructive method of directly measuring stress within a building element exists, but there is a minimally invasive technique that measures compressive stresses within masonry walls. A mortar joint is cut out and a "flat jack," which is a hydraulic jack thin enough to fit within the joint, is introduced into the wall. By pressurizing the jack, the amount of stress in the surrounding masonry can be determined. This technique is practical only for masonry walls and therefore is of no use in many situations.

Effective nondestructive testing of buildings often requires advanced equipment. Even as basic a measurement as gross building geometry is more accurate when performed with true surveying equipment (e.g., transits) than when performed solely with steel tapes. True surveyors' equipment is rarely needed for gross examination—a difference of a few inches per hundred feet should not affect a structural analysis—but if the difference in accuracy matters in an investigation, professional surveyors should be employed.

In some cases, the high-tech approach can eliminate probing. Geometric information often found using probes, such as rebar size and spacing, concrete voids, structural steel location, or steel beam depth, can sometimes be obtained using nondestructive techniques. Condition assessment, such as the thickness of rust on a steel spandrel beam, may or may not require visual observation, while some of the more complicated geometric information, such as rivet spacing, may simply be beyond the capacity of affordable technology.

At the simplest end of the spectrum of nondestructive testing is an ad-hoc, low-technology test such as sounding steel beams. This test consists of simply rapping an exposed steel beam with a steel hammer or piece of pipe. Solid steel will ring with a high (not necessarily musical) note, while beams with areas of delaminated rust will sound dead. This useful test is based on the ability of a homogeneous material to carry standing waves. A linear element such as a beam, where one dimension is much greater than the other two, will carry sound waves back and forth down its length unless the waves are interrupted by an imperfection in the geometry, such as an irregular patch of rust. Sounding is used with other materials, although the tests differ in their details. Sounding masonry (usually with a rubber mallet) is performed to determine voids through the hollow sound, while sounding wood with a hammer will indicate rot or insect damage through a dead sound in the area of the impact.

More advanced methods, such as x-ray, magnetic resonance, and ultrasonic testing, can determine more complicated information than the simple presence of steel. The condition of existing structure, including the presence of delaminated rust, voids from freezing during curing in concrete, and voids from weathering in masonry piers can be found. Unfortunately, these techniques require more time and expense than can ordinarily be expended on a renovation project. Their only extensive use to date has been in forensic investigations, where the need to find a cause of failure overrides cost considerations, and in the preservation and restoration of monuments, where saving the original material is of paramount importance.

Advanced testing

The most advanced and widely used (although not most informative) nondestructive test is sonic imaging. Sonic imaging uses the reflection of sound waves to locate voids, discontinuities, and changes in density in thick materials such as masonry and concrete. High-frequency sound waves ("ultrasonic" waves) can provide more detail, but are more easily deflected by large-scale discontinuities, such as an internal juncture between masonry types in a wall.

Radar imaging operates on the same basic principle as sonic imaging but substitutes the sound waves with shortwave radio. The capacity of the radio waves to pass through different structural materials differs, and radar may be significantly distorted by metal embedded in the structure.

Thermal imaging measures infrared radiation from a structure. It can distinguish small differences in temperature between portions of an element—for example, a heavy masonry wall. These thermal differences, in turn, can be correlated with internal discontinuities, previous alterations, and the presence of water or other damage. Because the temperature measurements are confined to the surface being measured, information hidden within the element may not be detected.

Magnetic resonance imaging uses magnets to locate the magnetic resistance typically caused by metals within an element. (Figure 9-1) Iron and steel are easiest to find using this technique, although aluminum and other metals can be detected. Extremely fine calibration is required if useful structural information, such as reinforcing rod size, is to be found; otherwise the simple presence or absence of metal and rough locations are what is detected.

X-ray imaging works on buildings in the same manner it is used in medicine: film placed on one side of an object captures x-ray radiation emitted from a controlled source on the other side. A picture of hidden elements is made. There are three drawbacks with extensive use of x-ray imaging in buildings: first, relatively high levels of radiation may be need-

9-1. Using a magnetic resonance scanner to locate steel beams, which are then marked with orange paint.

ed to penetrate structural materials, creating safety concerns in occupied buildings; second, the pictures produced are three dimensions "collapsed" into two and may be difficult to read; and third, the need for access to both sides combined with the relatively heavy and awkward equipment limits feasible locations for field use.

Earth testing

A more common form of nondestructive testing is the removal of earth to observe foundation conditions; earth testing is considered nondestructive because the earth being removed is not stressed. The easiest form of removal is performed in gross amounts through hand or backhoe digging of test pits. These methods can provide extensive subsurface data that may not have been available to the original designers of a building or that may have changed since the building was erected. Because the investigation is more than a simple examination for surface conditions—it detects the presence of ground water and the type of bearing material—it should be considered testing rather than observation. Test pits do not qualify as probes for two reasons: First, while the material extracted during a probe is seldom replaced, test pits are ordinarily filled in, because if they are left open they may become a source of damage to the building. Second, test pits are opened in part to examine the condition of the bearing stratum below footings—this determination is a judgment of the structural value of the earth rather than the simple measurement ordinarily resulting from probes.

Simple earth removal is related to two other techniques: bore drilling and archaeology. While test pits can be easily dug, they are severely limited in depth. Using specialized drilling equipment, bore drilling, even inside a cellar, can easily go through more than soil and therefore is usually subcontracted as other testing is. In urban settings, boring logs from previous testing may already exist for the property in question or for adjacent properties. While preexisting borings usually do not satisfy building-code requirements for borings for new construction, they may provide useful information on an existing design. If new borings are needed for examination of existing footings (an extremely rare procedure because of the expense and mess), they are taken by moving a drilling rig inside or next to the building in question. If old boring logs are being examined, the general documentation procedures described in chapter 6 apply.

Earth removal can also intersect archaeology, specifically industrial or urban archaeology. Most statutes for the landmarking of buildings contain provisions for examination of earth moved. Industrial archaeology thrives on old garbage, which can give a great deal of detailed information about its era and is commonly found in old foundation trenches, abandoned wells, and other filled-in excavations. Often during excavation for a new building, some kind of artifact (household objects, abandoned gravesites, old foundations or boundary walls) is found, triggering an archaeological investigation and shutting down the construction site. For this reason, builders hate to find artifacts because they interfere with construction scheduling. If renovations entail building new foundations, the archaeological issues are the same as with new construction. The presence of an archaeologist may be required during excavation if there is reason to believe that artifacts may be found.

Artifacts may be found during the digging of new foundation pits or of test pits used to examine the condition of footings and bearing strata. Since mass excavation rarely takes place in renovation (happening most frequently when a cellar floor is lowered to create additional headroom), the likelihood of mass archaeology is reduced. However, it may become an issue when test pits are dug inside very old buildings (1800 or earlier), as the foundation trenches of buildings have historically been one of the best sources of artifacts.

Movement

Investigations are often triggered because excessive movement of a building is suspected, especially when construction work is being performed nearby. Measurements of suspected movement are common tests in such cases.

As described earlier, it is normal for masonry buildings to have some degree of cracking. If there is any reason to believe that the cracks are actively moving, monitoring them is part of an ongoing investigation. Crack widths can be measured with a ruler, but this is not particularly accurate or repeatable, as different measurements (even if the measurement location is marked on the masonry) may not catch the same spot on the irregular edge of the crack. Various forms of crack monitor are available and fall into two broad categories: motion indicators and distance indicators. The first simply tells an investigator whether or not motion has taken place, while the second measures the distance moved.

Motion indicators do not require special tools: pieces of masking tape can serve as motion indicators, as can pencil lines drawn on walls. Since motion indicators may be in place and checked over a period of months, a better solution is one resistant to wind and water attack. Small glass tubes with a narrow neck are commercially available from builders' supply hardware manufacturers. The relatively thick ends of the tube are epoxied to a wall on either side of the crack. If movement takes place, the neck breaks. Obviously, glass indicators have to be placed where they will not come into contact with passersby or other physical impact.

The most common type of distance monitor consists of two pieces of plastic that are fastened to the masonry on opposite sides of the crack. The first piece is opaque and lies flat against the wall surface; the second is transparent and is mounted over the first piece. Each piece is marked with a small grid. The grids are aligned when the pieces are mounted, allowing for measurement of the grids relative to one another. (Figure 9-2) By checking the grid alignment at regular intervals (either once a day or once a week depending on the severity of the damage believed to be present), the investigator can develop a profile of any progressive movement.

9-2. A monitor mounted over a crack in a concrete slab floor in the same manner used for masonry walls. This picture was taken immediately after installation, so the crosshairs are centered.

Vibration

Building movement does not take place in a vacuum. Settlement is preceded or accompanied by vibrations and impacts, which can be measured separately from the overall movement. Even vibrations (from adjacent construction or another cause) too small to contribute to gross movement can cause damage. Vibration measurement is more comprehensive than movement measurement, since the vibrations detected include those too small to cause damage.

The basic piece of equipment to measure vibration is a form of seismograph. This is not a coincidence: vibration damage is caused by rapid back-and-forth acceleration of brittle materials (including plaster, masonry, glass, and even concrete)—this is basically a small-scale version of the damage caused by an earthquake. There is no clear difference between the damage caused by earthquakes and that caused by other forms of vibration. Relatively fragile buildings, such as poorly maintained rowhouses, have been damaged by the presence of a large pothole in the street nearby. As trucks hit the pothole edge, they create an impact that is transmitted to the building through the earth, causing vibrations within the structure.

The accepted form of measurement for vibration is the measurement of acceleration. Measurement of displacement does not provide an accurate picture of the possible severity of damage, since a large displacement over a long time may be less damaging than a small and rapid movement. Seismographs are designed to measure acceleration both laterally and vertically and thus can be used to measure the effect of building motion in the same way that they measure ground motion.

Environmental conditions

Much of the damage that occurs in buildings is caused by environmental stress—water entry and extremes of temperature. While visual examination can reveal damage and therefore provide an indirect measure of environmental stress, advanced testing is required to quantify the problems. Testing can also eliminate possible causes of known damage.

Thermal measurement can be as simple as taping a thermometer to a building and checking the reading on a regular basis. This technique is not often used because the locations in question may be inaccessible (e.g., inside walls) and because thermal measurements are best taken on a regular basis throughout the course of the daily temperature cycle as well as the yearly temperature cycle. Electronic thermometers can be placed once (many have long probes that can be inserted into small holes drilled in finishes) and hooked up to a recorder that provides a graph of temperature fluctuations on any given schedule. Regular temperature recording should be used for a specific purpose—large amounts of data can easily be generated but have no meaning unless they can be correlated with a damage mechanism (for example, thermal stress at a corner of a facade).

Moisture measurements can be taken in the same way. A probe is inserted into a drilled hole in a wall, ceiling, or structural member and attached to a recorder to provide a record of the moisture level and any fluctuations over time. Since this is often closely linked to temperature changes, some combination probes measure both states. The same caveat applies to moisture measurements as to temperature: testing should not take place without a clear picture of how the results will be used. While large amounts of accurate, tabulated data may look important, the results are of little value unless the testing has a defined purpose.

Conclusion

Buildings seem familiar to everyone and are, for most people, the largest man-made objects in their daily lives. We literally spend our lives in and around buildings, using them and altering them in small ways. Few people give much thought to the structure of the wall in an office before attaching hanging shelves, and in few cases does the structure of the building matter. On those occasions when something goes wrong—for instance, when the shelves fall off the wall—the problem is not seen as a building failure. The common practice of maintaining and making small changes to buildings can create the false impression that we understand all building issues regardless of scale or complexity.

Because buildings are so familiar, learning how to investigate them requires looking with fresh eyes. Professionals are often surprised by the details they find while investigating a given building, while nonprofessionals may find that the basic structure and systems of their buildings, no matter how familiar, are a mystery. At the same time, the purpose of an investigation is to explain, not to complicate. An investigation that concludes that there are ten possible causes for cracks in a wall or gives three structural systems that might be present is worse than no investigation at all, since time, money, and effort were spent in producing an essentially useless result.

A useful investigation focuses on the physical nature of the building. Beneath the architectural style, the structure determines the use and condition of the building and therefore demands the most attention during investigation.

No matter how much high technology may be used in the construction of a building (such as computer-aided design) or in systems within the building (such as electronic controls on air-conditioning systems), the solid physical reality of walls and floors remain the overriding public perception of construction. Everyone has seen a brick wall and in some way understands it. In comparison, relatively few people understand the electronics embedded in an automobile engine. As the physical artifacts of our everyday experience have become more complicated—and particularly as they have moved from mechanical, to electrical, to electronic operation—the technology has become more distant from the people who use it. The structure of buildings has not been part of this trend because the nature of the function—supporting load against gravity, wind, and other forces—cannot be moved from the physical realm to a virtual one. Building systems, on the other hand, have been part of this trend—for example, in the twentieth century mechanical controllers for elevators were replaced first by electric controllers and then by far more complicated electronic controls.

Despite the necessary emphasis on system and logic, investigating buildings can be as fascinating as a mystery story. One of the goals of an investigation is, after all, to figure out what the designers and builders were thinking years before. An understanding of a building's original design, whether arrived at by examination of documents showing the design intent or by analysis of the structure itself, is the soundest basis for making decisions about the building's future. Purchase decisions, alteration feasibility, alteration design, and repair design can all proceed without an investigation, but only at great expense and with a probability of delays due to unforeseen conditions.

Pre-purchase Investigations

Pre-purchase investigations are often called "due diligence" investigations for their role in the legal process of ownership transfer. The prospective purchaser has the opportunity to investigate the building for damage or lack of code compliance because the contract of sale usually states that the purchaser accepts the building condition as is.

These investigations often begin in total ignorance of the nature and condition of building systems, and are usually limited by time and access. As the investigator is working for a prospective owner and not the actual owner, disruptive and destructive work such as large-scale removal of dropped ceilings and probing is not usually possible. Certain areas of the building, for example those occupied by sensitive tenants, may be off-limits to the investigator. This limitation is partially compensated by limited scope: pre-purchase investigation reports are focused on identifying existing and potential problems and providing schematic repair recommendations.

The report becomes one of the documents reviewed by the purchaser in making the final decision to proceed. It is possible, but not usual, that a pre-purchase report will be directly used in repair work following the sale. More often, the report becomes the basis for a more detailed maintenance investigation of those areas flagged as current or potential problems. Obviously, there are differing degrees of concern, and problems identified as dangerous or likely to require expensive repairs are the ones most likely to stop a sale and to be further investigated if the sale goes ahead.

Maintenance Investigations

The size and complexity of even small buildings combined with the relentless effects of weathering and gravity ensure that no building is ever in perfect condition. In a well-kept building, maintenance issues may be of small importance and unnoticeable to the occupants, but periodic investigations of condition are still necessary because of the progressive and accelerating nature of most weather damage. Maintenance investigation differs from pre-purchase and alteration investigation most in that they are ordinarily conducted by people familiar with the building systems and history—either maintenance staff or professionals who have dealt with the building before. These investigations are not required by a specific condition at the time, but rather they are triggered by a known problem, by a specific schedule for investigation, or by code requirements.

Maintenance investigation may not produce formal reports, because they are focused on recommendations for repair of problems found in the context of known relatively stable conditions. In an extreme example, the only report may be a short memo describing locations of the most recent occurrences of a chronic problem, such as leaking shower bodies in an apartment house. Even if the reports are this simple, or consist of simple maintenance required forms, they should be kept together in an organized manner, as they constitute an important source of information for other, larger-scale investigations.

Alteration Investigations

Depending on the type of alteration considered for a building, the timing of an investigation may vary. If design is dependent on the structural or mechanical feasibility of a given scheme (usually when large-scale ideas like removing columns are combined with small-scale budgets), then the investigation must be performed during schematic design. If the basics of the building are known and the proposed alteration is relatively simple (for example, installing a tenant stair in a modern steel-frame building), then the investigation can usually wait until the last stages of design.

Depending on the scale of the alteration proposed, the scope of investigation can vary widely. Many small alterations have a one-visit investigation performed to confirm assumptions made by the designers—for example, that certain partitions are not load bearing, or that an apparently abandoned plumbing branch can be removed. In these cases, the investigation report is often simply a memo confirming the assumptions and providing the logical basis for moving forward with construction.

Large changes in the building systems or use may require an investigation from top to bottom of all mechanical and structural elements. Such investigations may take weeks and often produce detailed reports that describe the existing systems in depth with plan drawings barely distinguishable from construction documents. The report becomes the basis for design and construction.

Afterwards

All of the process and details of investigation described here have meaning only as long as the conclusions of the investigation are used. One of the more frustrating experiences for design professionals is to conduct an investigation and then have the resulting report disappear from view because the building owner or manager disagrees with the conclusions and recommendations. Fortunately, few people are so irresponsible as to ignore reports that their buildings are unsafe.

An investigation is part of the life cycle of a building. The most common types of investigation are those conducted as part of a purchase, those performed as part of an alteration, and those conducted at the beginning of a new maintenance cycle. The individual steps performed and the technical information sought are very similar, with only a difference in emphasis distinguishing one type from the others. Since most buildings are sold more than once between construction and demolition, develop problems requiring repair more than once, and are altered in some way more than once, all three types of investigation are likely to be performed on a typical building,

A POCKET CHECKLIST FOR INVESTIGATORS

Regardless of building type, the basic steps of an investigation are

- Identify building type and systems
- Identify and prioritize damage by looking for movement, material deterioration, and identifying load conditions
- Document field conditions
- Carry out on-site probes and testing if required

Identify and classify damage by asking such questions as

- Is the damage worse at the top of the building than at the bottom?
- Is it worse at the bottom than at the top?
- Are cracks diagonal, vertical, horizontal, or a combination of directions?
- Is the damage located primarily on one face of the building, on opposing faces, or on adjacent faces?
- Does the damage appear to be active (ongoing) at the time of the investigation or does it seem to have taken place in the past? Are the edges of cracks sharp (new) or rounded (old)?
- Have cracks widened, indicating movement in one direction, or do they seem to be working back and forth (opening and closing over time)?
- What is the load history of the building?
- What are the local conditions outside of the building (microclimate)
- Do exposures face water or open land?
- Have there been changes in the microclimate?
- Are there neighboring buildings?
- Has the arrangement of neighboring buildings changed?

Check views on site

- From the roof
- From the surrounding streets and grounds
- From neighboring roofs
- From mid-air (scaffolding)
- Within exterior rooms
- In public halls
- Within interior rooms

Identify technical architectural features

- Exterior wall types
- Roof types

Identify structural system types

- Masonry bearing walls
- Wood- and steel-joist floors
- Masonry vault floors

- Heavy-timber frames
- Wood stud
- Steel stud
- Steel frame
- Concrete frame

Review mechanical systems

- Plumbing
- Drainage
- Gas
- Electricity
- Lighting
- Heating and boilers
- Ventilation
- Air-conditioning and chillers
- Fire-protection sprinklers
- Elevators

Research existing documentation

- Original design drawings
- Original shop drawings
- Drawings from alterations
- Drawings from previous investigations
- Reports from previous investigations
- Original construction photographs
- Photographs or videos from previous investigations

Destructive tests

- Probing
- Destructive testing of material samples
- Load testing
- Flood testing

Non-destructive tests

- Flat-jack stress tests
- Sounding
- Sonic, thermal, magnetic resonance, or x-ray imaging
- Test pits and borings
- Crack monitoring
- Vibration monitoring
- Thermal and moisture monitoring

Index

on-site work, 13–14
process, 10–11
scale of investigation,
    168–69
timing of investigation,
    168
documentation
    of damaged areas to be
        repaired, 119
    photographs and pictures,
        109–10, 112–13
    of probes, 150–52
    sources, 107–8
    thoroughness, 114–15
    types of, 103
    written reports, 108–9,
        113–15
    see also drawings
double beams, 104–5
drainage system, 80–81
drawings
    abbreviations in, 105,
        113–14
    creating, 110–12, 115–16
    degree of detail, 121–22
    erection plans, 107
    lettering style, 105
    limitations of, 39–41
    materials descriptions, 106
    need for, 32–33
    reading old originals,
        103–7
    verification, 106–7
ductwork, 86–87

E
earth testing, 160–62
education and training, 8, 9,
    12
    architects, 10
    engineers, 10–12
    for lab testing, 154
electrical system, 77
    basic features, 82
    heating, 84
    investigation, 82–83
    lighting, 83
element(s)
    defined, 17
    interaction, 30–31
elevators, 91
engineers/engineering

in historic preservation, 12
on-site work, 13–14
professional training for
    investigations, 10–12
environmental concerns
    buried oil tanks, 92
    measurement of environ-
        mental effects, 164
escalators, 91
exterior walls
    investigation examples,
        127–30, 133
    steel-frame buildings, 72
    stress evaluation, 95–97
    structural types, 46–47
    visual examination, 36–37

F
facades
    interaction of elements,
        31
    investigation examples,
        127–28, 133
fan-coil heating/cooling, 84,
    88
fieldwork. *see* on-site work
fire safety
    alarm systems, 90
    heavy timber construc-
        tion, 59
    sprinkler systems, 89–90
    wood joist construction,
        54–56
    wood-stud buildings, 64
flashing, 49
flood testing, 157
floors
    concrete joist, 66–67, 71,
        74
    concrete plank, 71
    concrete-slab, 57–58, 65,
        69–71
    masonry, 53, 56, 67–68,
        131–32
    steel beam, 56–57
    in steel-frame buildings,
        66–72
    steel joist, 56
    wood-joist, 53–56
foundations
    concrete, **98**
    earth testing, 160–62

masonry, 51, 52
wood-stud houses, 61–63
freeze-thaw cycle(s), 18
    block construction, 62
fuses, electrical, 82

G
gas system, 81
group-built houses, 62

H
half-timbered construction,
    59
hazardous materials, 126
heating system, 83–85
    air-conditioning system
        and, 88
    buried oil tanks, 91–92
Historic American Building
    Survey, 33
Historic American Engi-
    neering Record, 33
historic restorations, 8–9
    contextual considerations,
        16–17
    engineering issues, 12–13
    preservation vs. replace-
        ment of materials,
        15–16
history of a building
    documentation, 103–10
    memories of individuals
        about, 41
    as subject of investigation,
        7, 8

I
identification of building
    system, 20–21
indoor air quality, 86
insulation, 64
interaction of building ele-
    ments, 30
interior rooms, 37
interviews, 41
intuition, 39
investigation process
    field documentation,
        110–15
    principle activities, 19–20
    steps, 9
    structural damage, 93–98